MW00717301

Why we Act the way we do

How we Talk about it

Patricia Parvin Danks, PhD

Patricia Danks

Copyright © 2013

All rights reserved. No part of this publication may be reproduced, stored in a retrieval system, or transmitted, in any format or by any means, digital, electronic, mechanical, photocopying, recording, or otherwise, or conveyed via the Internet or Web site without written permission of Patricia Parvin Danks, except in the case of brief quotations embedded in critical articles and reviews.

Printed in the United States of America

ISBN: 97809892518-0-8
Library of Congress Control Number: 2013911182

Publisher's Cataloging-in-Publication Data

Danks, Patricia Parvin.
Why we act the way we do : how we talk about it / Patricia Parvin Danks.
p. cm.
Includes bibliographical references.
ISBN 978-0-98-925180-8
1. Conduct of life. 2. Interpersonal communication. 3. Self-actualization (Psychology).
I. Title.

158.1—dc23 2013911182

Edited by Penny Schreiber

Cover design, book layout, and illustrations by Nancy Rabitoy

www.patriciadanks.com

To my mother, Mary Moriarty Kenny,
who shared with me her insatiable love of reading.

Contents

Preface

My purpose in writing this book is to provide for the average reader a perspective on communication that is based in behavior. Readers can access many excellent resources if their desire is to improve their speaking skills. But in my work as a therapist I find that this is not enough for most people who are struggling with serious conflict in their lives. To communicate well, it is essential that we understand ourselves as well as the other person or persons we are engaging with. This is commonly expressed as: *I want to know where you're coming from* or *I want them to know who I am.* Most of us strive to be understood and to understand others, but without understanding behavior, we do not succeed at this so well.

My hope is that this book will rekindle the fire of good conversation in families and among friends. Although we spend many hours every week sharing sports, watching television, and interacting online, I fear we are losing the ability to express ourselves. When we cannot use our common language well, we are less likely to enter into a mature conversation. When we do not master thc art of conversation, we cannot represent ourselves. A lack of communication skills can hold us back from meeting important personal goals. Finally, the ability to express ourselves well plays a major role in achievement.

Throughout this book I have pulled from my personal experiences with family, friends, and clients. All of my stories have been altered to change names and other specifics. I have attempted to focus on a pattern of behavior or style of communication rather than on the actual persons involved.

Most of the concepts in this book are summarized at the end of each chapter. I recognize that couples coming for therapy, or who are using this book as a guide for discussion between them, have busy lives. A quick review of the information in the chapter summaries or the sidebars, while not ideal, can allow for a reasonable discussion.

Nuts and Bolts: To make my writing gender inclusive and avoid the confusion of deciding which pronouns are appropriate, I have randomly used *he* and *she* throughout. In a few instances where statistics or my professional experience suggest a behavior is most commonly associated with one gender, I have used that gender. In any case, my aim is to avoid as much as possible being gender specific and to get around the clunkiness of *he/she* or *her/him.*

Introduction

I have been in practice as a marriage and family therapist since 1985. During that time, I have met with well over a thousand people who have shared with me their personal and intimate experiences and life situations. Some of their stories have had common themes that reflect the experiences of many of us. Others have told me of their struggles with unusual and heartbreaking events that most of us will never experience. I have laughed and cried with my clients, often simultaneously. I honor the stories of my clients' struggles to survive emotionally and maintain their will to live.

During these thirty years, I have grappled with the trends that come in waves to challenge all of us who seek to live peaceful, productive lives. In the early 1980s I sat with parents agonizing over how to support children coming out as homosexuals. I shared tears with a generation of couples who having married as teenagers felt lost or cheated after a decade of adhering to a commitment they made long before they became adults. I helped many young people wade through the sexual revolution, and I supported their families as they struggled to tolerate their children's desire to live together without a marital commitment. Parents who have lost children in horrific accidents or homicidal assaults have sat frozen before me, too traumatized to speak or cry.

I have struggled with my clients to understand addiction as an illness and sort out which treatments are available and most effective for each individual person. In the 1990s and 2000s sexual addiction became a significant presenting problem in my practice. Like most of my colleagues, I've spent many hours in continuing education to learn the effects of this addiction, its impact on families, and, most important, a treatment that is effective for repairing the damage to the individual and his relationships. Numerous individuals have trusted me with stories of their families and childhoods as they unravel memories of abuse and neglect and attempt to construct a sense of identity and self-worth.

My work has been a blessing to me and, I suspect, to many who have found me on their journey to wellness. Together we have made marvelous progress. After all these years during which I have been privileged to share the heartbreak and joy of my clients, why have I chosen now to write a book on communication?

Perhaps it is a little late in coming, but I have wanted a book that I can hand to a client, a student, a teacher, or an employer that will explain the process of communication in terms that can be readily grasped and are helpful to others in resolving communication issues and enhancing relationships. A plethora of resources exist that encourage and instruct people on how to communicate. Most companies, churches, and professional groups sponsor in-service programs to provide communication skills to their members. Yet, in my experience, most people I meet do not know how to talk with one another. The people I meet are interested in making a change. They are faced with a problem or conflict or are experiencing distress with someone to whom they are close. But they are not aware of the significant role that communication makes in resolving their particular situation. And, typically, they are not aware of the role communication plays in bringing about positive changes in themselves that can affect their relationships at home and at work.

It is my belief that a lack of communication skills is the primary reason that marriages and other relationships fail. Common reasons that couples divorce include financial problems, infidelity, immaturity, or a tragic event such as the death of a child. But experience tells us that couples can, and do, get through all of these challenges. Often, with guidance, a marriage becomes stronger after the couple walk together through these fires of life. It is their inability to communicate about the experiences they share that destroys their relationship. Many couples cannot connect with the appropriate words to express feelings and comfort each other; nor can they effectively discuss and resolve a serious issue. The same holds true for employers and employees. When a person is aware of how his actions affect others and he can express himself in an open format, he will be more likely to resolve issues with co-workers in a direct manner. Responsible communication can go a long way toward reducing destructive backbiting and office gossip.

When parents hear and respect the experiences and feelings of their children, conflict will be lessened in their home. Many people learn to live with angry outbursts or unrealistic expectations and threats and, therefore, cannot speak up for themselves. This may also leave them unable to express encouragement, fear, love, and concern.

Adults caring for aging parents cause themselves unnecessary grief because they cannot tell their parents how they feel or what they will be able or not able to do for them. When caregivers say no to an elderly parent they often feel shame, fearing they have betrayed their loved one. Sometimes they jeopardize their own health or neglect family needs for fear they will hurt their parent's feelings. All of these dynamics can improve when a caregiver has a better understanding of herself and can untangle her feelings of love and allegiance from her feelings of resentment and fatigue and fear of loss.

It is not uncommon for me to meet a couple who have been married for years and have never discussed their sexual relationship with each other. It isn't that they do not want to talk about it, they just do not know how. It is surprising how little couples know about their own sexuality. Many never express their thoughts because they are not sure what is "normal." Yet they can become highly verbal when I open the conversation and introduce new information and a workable vocabulary. I've learned that it is difficult for many people to express themselves well, especially when talking about something controversial or personal, especially if it is something intimate.

Often clients sit with me and explain that they are coming to me after a year or more of therapy they have found unhelpful, and they complain that it was a waste of time. They begin their work with me by blaming their spouse or family member or someone else for their feelings and behavior. Or they may be at a loss because they do not know how to say what they need to say. Or they are afraid to ask for what they need or want. I question what they did in months of therapy when they then come to me with no ability to speak for themselves. In all the years of my work counseling individuals, couples, and families, I have encountered only a few clients with adequate enough communication skills to navigate a problem to resolution.

I quickly learned that therapy is most successful when the art of communication is the primary focus during the early sessions. Without these skills, a person cannot describe a problem behavior without blaming another and defending himself. Because each person is determined that the other is the cause of his bad feelings, he projects his frustration, resentment, disappointment, or other negative feelings away from himself and onto another. It is common for a couple to repeat the same argument for years, regenerating feelings of hurt and resentment, and creating even more distance between them. However, with a little direction and some communication skills, most couples can learn how to resolve a disagreement without arguing. They must be able to recognize the ways they each contribute to the stalemate between them. They must learn that each has the power to change. Once the situation is understood, they often find their way to compatible views by expressing their individual points clearly and responsibly. Once effective skills have been introduced, the couple can often work out the problem without further guidance.

It concerns me that verbal communication is becoming more difficult as people spend less time in face-to-face conversation and more time texting, talking to one another on social networks, and using e-mail. I certainly use and appreciate the convenience of all of these perks of modern life, but I worry that people are losing the ability to feel comfortable around others. So many today are overcome with stress, and sometimes panic, when they face an interview with a potential employer or are asked to speak before even a small group of people. Virtual communication, via telephone or online, can deprive a person of the physical experience of being present while interacting with others. Being physically present with another person allows for facial expression, eye contact, voice intonation, and body movement that add character and emphasis to conversation. It also allows the speaker to feel the discomfort of bringing his body into the conversation. For instance, he must decide what to do with his hands, control the urge to fidget, and try to avoid feeling physically awkward.

I do realize that technology is being updated faster than I can keep up with it, and it is common today to be able to use visual tools to see the person you are speaking with in real time. But will this really take the place of getting together physically?

How to communicate well is not difficult to learn, but unlearning miscommunication can be very difficult. Some of the rules of speaking that are taught to children do not work so well in adulthood. Today parents and educators encourage young children to use proper words to describe their feelings and experiences, sometimes in more than one language. This trend is helpful in preventing the need to unlearn poor communication habits and patterns later.

In the past, unspoken rules existed about what not to say or what not to talk about. Many still hold to the common practice of avoiding politics, sex, and religion. I wonder if this is practical today. Our world seems to be getting smaller and more diverse. In a twenty-four-hour period, we may be cyber-exposed to an unlimited array of situations, cultures, and languages. We will need to communicate with one another in order to make life work.

Maybe we do need to discuss politics and religion, especially with those who hold differing views. Because political and religious views weave together in so many ways, wouldn't it be better if people could express their ideas without the fear of verbal attack, interruption, or criticism? Can we learn to be quiet and listen to another person even when we disagree? Can we learn to hear another's views without judging their opinions to be unworthy of consideration? Have we beaten down the possibility of an exchange of ideas and replaced it with the notion that *I am right and if you disagree with me, there is something wrong with you, and I have the right to insult you by talking over you and yelling at you.* This behavior is common in the media and even in families.

Realistically, couples and families and co-workers are forced to live with their differences, knowing they may never agree. It is not unusual for couples to practice different religions or to not practice any religion. As children reach young adulthood, they often explore a faith different from their parents'. It is not uncommon for several political persuasions to be represented in a family or marriage or among close friends. With open dialogue, these differences need not hamper relationships. There is much to be respected in those who decide to *agree to disagree* and learn to *live with their differences.* But even this approach is a form of communication. For those who cannot or do not want to tolerate diversity, it is probably best that they stick to discussing the weather.

As suggested by its title, this book is divided into two sections: Part I offers a basic formula for understanding, evaluating, and choosing behavior. It defines the perceptions, truths, beliefs, and feelings that produce behavior. It offers the reader a working definition of behavior, its development in human history, and the manner in which the average human being behaves in today's world. The relationship between the brain and behavior will be introduced. The reader will understand the need to assess and understand her own behavior and make positive change. She will be able to recognize when to change her behavior in order to effect change in a marriage, family, or social group. The reader will have the ability to choose and develop a behavior style that allows her to function with others at a higher level.

Much of this writing is focused on a change of perception for the reader. When basic skills are mastered, I predict my readers will realize that it is reasonable and possible to communicate well. Communication can be difficult to learn because we have been conditioned to focus on the other as the source of both our happiness and misery: *If only* he *would change, if only* they *would change, how happy I would be.* For many readers, changing one's own behavior, when the other is the cause of the problem, will be a new concept.

It is imperative that a person understand when they cannot expect change or a positive response from others. It would be unfair to leave the reader with the impression that this process will appeal to everyone or that every person is willing or able to change his behavior. People who suffer from severe personality disorders, such as borderline personality disorder and dependent personality disorder, cannot be expected to change the way they behave. This does not mean they cannot change, but it is not likely that they will do so without professional help. With treatment, their behavior can be stabilized, but long-term positive change is not to be expected. Likewise, persons with untreated affective disorders, such as moderate to severe anxiety, depression, or bipolar disorder, most likely will not change or are not motivated to change their behavior. And those persons with untreated addictions are not good candidates for change. Be aware, though, that people with these difficult diagnoses can make dramatic, long-term change with proper support and treatment.

Another disorder that presents all too often in families is antisocial personality disorder. A person who manifests this disorder is commonly known as a sociopath or psychopath. Many people associate the word "sociopath" with long-term inpatient care, imprisonment, and serial murder. However, we have learned that sociopaths are very much a part of our social structure. Their abusive behavior continues to shape the lives of children, marriages, and communities. Since the behavior of the sociopath is a major cause of dysfunction and chaos in a home, workplace, and other social environments, this disorder is addressed further in Chapter 1.

Part II introduces basic communication skills. It presents a model of communication that can help the reader learn to discuss his behavior, views, and experiences in an interesting manner that will invite a mature response from the other. The reader will learn a responsible communication style that can prevent him from becoming ensnared in an argument or other unproductive or harmful exchanges. He will recognize communication cues that lead him to dysfunctional communication patterns. With recognition of these destructive patterns, the reader will learn new ways to communicate that are more effective and acceptable. The reader will learn to speak assertively and truthfully without threatening or challenging the other, unless threat or challenge is his intent.

This information is presented so that it can be easily understood by teens as well as adults. When adults model mature and responsible behavior, children feel safe and confident and better about themselves, and their behavior will reflect this. With competent skills, children, like anyone, can be ready to tackle adult-size problems that sometimes come early in their life. It is my hope that the ideas and guidelines presented here will be used in family and social interactions, business settings, and in the therapy consulting room.

Part One

WHY WE ACT THE WAY WE DO

Chapter 1

Understanding Behavior

Shaped a little like a loaf of French country bread, our brain is a crowded chemistry lab, bustling with nonstop neural conversations.

Diane Ackerman, American poet and naturalist

The brain

Behavior, simply stated, is the manner in which a person conducts himself. Anything an organism does in response to its environment is considered behavior. Behavior is an action-response to stimulation in the brain. Humans have a triune brain, which means one brain that is constituted by three separate brains that evolved separately at different times in human history. Each performs specific and interdependent functions, and together the three areas constitute what is known as the human brain.

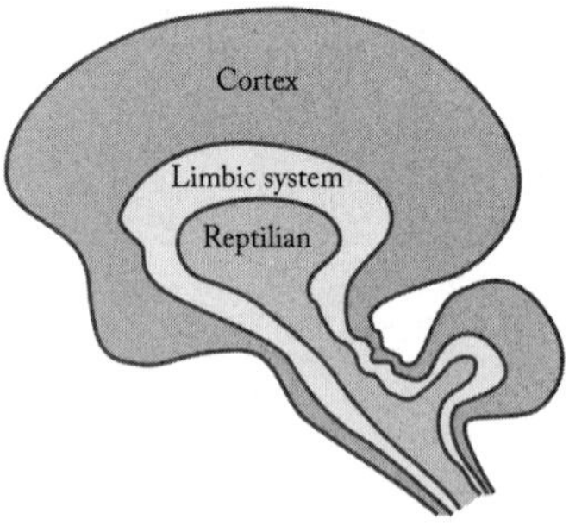

The first brain is the oldest of the three. Because it is not very different from the brain of reptiles, it is known as *R Complex*. The function of R Complex is to keep an organism safe, defending itself and its territory. It manages basic drives and instincts that allow the organism to survive in its environment. It attends to needs like hunger, sleep, and regulation of body temperature, which are body functions that protect the organism and allow it to thrive and reproduce. In humans, it is this brain that regulates the ability to respond to a stimulus without thinking and reasoning. It is this first brain that stimulates a hand to pull away from a hot surface without requiring the individual to think about the danger and make a conscious decision. It regulates an activity response without engaging thought or reason. When a person acts impulsively this process is involved. His behavior is a reaction to a threat, craving, instinct, sound, emotional or physical pain, or other stimulation.

Although this process is not adequate for solving problems or setting goals, it is this primitive brain that stimulates a mother to catch a toddler who starts to fall or stimulates a person to duck or put his arms up to protect against a flying object. Reacting to the environment in a protective way is a normal human behavior and one of the oldest and most primitive behaviors. While the R Complex brain is vital in providing humans with the ability to react quickly, it is not enough for us to maintain life at a higher level of functioning. Acting without thinking (acting impulsively) is a behavior pattern that is vital for survival, but it can also lead to chaos and possible danger for humans.

The second brain, the *limbic* system, evolved in animals 120 to 350 million years ago. It developed in a way that created an arc around the R Complex. The limbic system takes its name from *limbus,* the Latin word for border or margin. This more recently evolved part of the brain is similar to the brains of other animals that are considered old species, such as dogs, cats, and horses. Observing the difference in behavior between a pet snake and the family dog or between a bird and a mouse will illustrate that the species with the more developed brain, the dog and mouse, functions at a higher level and has a wider range of behaviors than reptiles and birds. The limbic system also allows humans the ability to function at a higher level than does the R-Complex. This second brain is the center for receiving and interpreting sensory impulses and transmitting information to the muscles and body organs. It is this center that communicates emotion, memory, and sensory perception to other parts of the brain as well. With this brain system, humans can send memories of sensations to the cortex for future reference and processing. As sensations combine with emotions, they are relayed to the cortex for cognitive interpretation.

The third brain is known as the *cortex* and is similar to the brain of other mammals. Since this brain is the newest part of the mammalian brain, it covers the first two brains like a cap. It is the cortex that regulates higher functions seen only in primates. In humans the cortex is much larger than that of other primates and is believed to have developed in association with the development of language. It is the cortex that enables humans to reflect on and assess a situation, choose a behavior, and plan a response. Humans' cognitive ability is regulated and made possible by this most recently evolved third brain. Note that each of these parts of the human brain acts in concert with the other two. This is a very simple explanation of an extremely complicated process that involves all parts of the brain. However, it will suffice for our discussion here and will help distinguish between *reactive* and *responsive* behavior.

Consider the following: Whether someone reacts without thinking or makes a thoughtful decision in choosing his response is his choice. When he decides to make a positive change in his behavior, it is imperative that he know the difference between being reactionary or *response-able.* The person who feels the sensation and acts on it without engaging a higher level of functioning is reacting or acting without thinking. But when someone thinks about or reflects on the stimulus before acting, he makes a responsible choice about the way he will respond. He engages conscious intention.

In Summary: One area in the brain senses danger and transmits it to another area. When the sensation is received, it is interpreted and produces emotion, such as excitement or fear. The emotion is then transmitted to the cortex, where interpretation and reflection on the meaning of the sensation or emotion occurs. A decision is then made about the external event. Again, I remind the reader that this is a simplistic description. The movements and responses in the brain are not limited to this definition and involve infinitely more complicated dynamics.

Chapter 2

Behavior Change

As human beings, our greatness lies not so much in being able to remake the world . . . as in being able to remake ourselves.

Mahatma Gandhi, Indian spiritual leader

The need to belong

Nobody likes to be embarrassed or to feel badly about their behavior. Perhaps most people want to be good. They want others to think well of them and do not want others to see their faults and shortcomings. Humans are social creatures who need to depend on and be in relationships with other humans. People do not typically do well on their own, thriving best when interacting with others at some level. Until recent history, to be left alone or abandoned meant sure death. One person could not survive for long against the threats of the environment without the support of a tribe or community. While this threat to survival may not be true for all people today, the archetypal, or classic, fear of being alone or excluded is still with us. It is this fear that makes us react, or overreact, to rejection by others.

People want to be liked by others—we thrive when accepted and included in a social circle of support. Because people need the support and friendship of other humans, we tend to shape our behavior in relationship to others. Other people are like mirrors, reflecting our actions back to us. Sometimes a person will feel uncomfortable and go to great lengths to be loved and accepted by others. Another may only find comfort when she can control her family or social group to act in a way that benefits her, helping her to feel safe.

Whether or not we are accepted or rejected by society, our brain produces a strong emotion. Either our environment is threatened and we sense harm or our environment is nonthreatening and we feel secure. When areas of the cortex receive this emotional message, it is interpreted and an appropriate behavior is selected. All people have had some experience of rejection and felt deeply hurt. The initial hurt is irrational and the result of raw emotion. If a person acts at this level, her behavior will be reactionary, and she is more likely to strike out at the perceived threat. For example:

> *When Lily and Stanley planned to be married, they looked at several options in planning their celebration. They have many relatives and friends and quickly realized that a large gathering that included all of their friends and loved ones would be costly and unwieldy. Neither wanted to spend their money on a state-of-the art wedding and devote their time to such an event. Instead, they decided on a small elegant ceremony on the beach in Maui. They invited only their parents, explaining to brothers and sisters, nieces and nephews, aunts and uncles, cousins and friends that they would have a reception at home the following week.*

Lily and Stanley were not prepared for the responses they received. Many who were not invited to the wedding ceremony felt hurt and rejected. E-mails and telephone calls came by the dozens asking for an explanation: *What did I do? Why wasn't I invited?* People were certain that it was a personal dislike or rejection that excluded them. Some who were feeling the emotional pain of rejection had the ability to reflect on the situation and consider several possibilities: 1) *Weddings can be very expensive. Lily and Stanley have many friends and family members who want to celebrate with them. This is what they want and it is their choice, and I'm OK with that,* or 2) *They could have invited me and I could have paid my fare to Hawaii; it would not need to be so costly for them*, or 3*) Lily and Stanley are selfish and do not really care about their family and friends. I am going to let them know in some way how hurt I am.*

The manner in which their brains process the feeling of hurt will determine the action each person will take. In Lily and Stanley's example, most of their family and friends wished them well and planned to attend the reception and celebrate with them. A very few people still remember and feel the hurt of not being invited, mistakenly believing that it was personal and they were not wanted at the celebration.

Because people feel both security and threat in relation to others, they believe that others are the source of their feelings. It is true that external stimuli do initiate a primitive level of emotion, but a feeling is produced when the brain processes the emotion. A feeling results from the brain's ability to reason. In the example given above, a person who reacted to the emotion caused by rejection is more likely to present a cold face to the couple and avoid the reception. They might avoid the couple altogether, nursing the negative emotion and choosing to think: *They are selfish and they don't care about me. They're not real friends.* On the other hand, those who used reason to quiet the emotion will experience a manageable feeling of loss, along with peace and acceptance, allowing for a continued relationship with Lily and Stanley.

People experience pain and pleasure in relationship to their environment. The natural tendency is to look for someone or something that causes their feelings of pleasure and pain. A person who is looking to someone else—a spouse, a baby, a friend—to make her happy may never find what she wants. It is just not true that one person can make another happy. It is classic for people to think they will be happy if they have more money or a beautiful home or a relaxing vacation. Yet most know this is not true. Lasting happiness does not come from outside but is the result of an individual's state of mind. When the focus is directed toward looking out, instead of looking in, people tend to believe that others are the cause of their feelings or their problems. This false perception will change as a person achieves emotional maturity. As one leaves childhood and approaches adulthood, he learns that, with few exceptions, each person is responsible for the way she thinks and behaves. Emotional pain and pleasure are the result of an ability, or inability, to rationally process stimuli and emotion. Responsible human behavior is a result of an inner process and is not caused by others or something outside of one's self. It is the result of engaging the full brain in processing and choosing a response, instead of reacting to the stimuli manifested in the limbic system.

When the other will not change

Many people will not change their behavior simply because they do not want to. It is common to hear a client or a spouse say, *I have a bad temper, just like my mom—she had meltdowns all the time* or *I've always been lazy, and I'm just like my father—he came home from work and drank beer and watched television every night. I come by it honestly.* These statements are an announcement that these individuals have accepted the behavior they've observed in others and have adopted it as their own. They do not realize that they can decide to behave differently.

If you are unwilling to change your behavior, you will be unable to solve many of your problems. To solve a problem, a person must first own the problem or accept that the problem is his.

Next, he must change his behavior to fix the problem. This statement generally evokes resistance until it is understood. A person can only solve his own problem. But how do you know whether the problem is yours or someone else's? Believe it or not, the problem belongs to the one that feels bad. Alcoholics Anonymous has taught us much about owning our own behavior. Let us look at the Wilson family to get a better understanding:

> *Alicia, the mother, has had a drinking problem for several years. She is a stay-at-home mom who relaxes at lunch with a glass of red wine. By 2:30, when her teenage daughter comes home, she has had one or two more glasses. Although she does not seem intoxicated when her daughter arrives, she is guarded and somewhat detached. Her twelve-year-old son arrives home and asks to go to a friend's home. Alicia does not have the energy or attention to spend time with him and is grateful that he has a safe place to go. She encourages him to do his homework and, since she is not needed, she has another small glass of wine. At 6, when her husband arrives home, the family has dinner without their son, who has decided to eat with his friend's family. After dinner Alicia falls asleep on the sofa. Her daughter goes to her room and talks with friends online. Her son comes home at 10 and goes to bed. Her husband visits with a neighbor until midnight and then goes to bed. Alicia comes to bed about an hour later.*

At first glance we think Alicia has the problem. It might seem obvious that Alicia needs to make major changes in her behavior. But the odds are in her favor. She does not believe she has a problem and is actually quite comfortable with her lifestyle. Alicia is confident that her son is safe and in a good environment. She knows from past experience that he will get his homework finished and keep up his grades. Her daughter seems happy because she does not complain and spends her time isolated in her room—a good girl, she is no bother to Alicia. And her husband seems happy visiting with the neighbor. Everything is going well in Alicia's little world. She might even celebrate with another glass of wine.

So who has the problem? Her daughter feels ignored and thinks her mother is not interested in her activities. She has stopped talking with her about the challenges and excitement of high school. Her son is disengaging from the home; he is identifying instead with the warmth and affirmation of another family. Her husband is finding friendship with a neighbor and feels shut out by his wife. Their relationship has changed, and their emotional and sexual intimacy faded months ago. Alicia is unaware of how her family feels about her. To expect her to change of her own volition is unrealistic, because she does not see the problems. Her drinking must somehow become a problem for her. She must feel badly before she will consider changing.

When each member of Alicia's family confronts their problems of feeling distanced, ignored, cheated, and lonely, Alicia might begin to feel badly herself and just might decide to change. For instance, if her husband begins an emotional or physical affair, she might feel threatened enough to wake up to the problem. If her daughter seeks emotional support and friendship from the wrong friend, she might realize that her daughter is disengaged. Her fears for her daughter might make her change. Or if her son decides he would rather live with his friend's family, she might realize that she has shut him out. This is the purpose of interventions: when loved ones confront the individual who is causing the problem and explain that they are going to change their own behavior to solve the problem, and the solution causes pain for the offender, then the offender may decide to make a change.

The bottom line is that one person cannot make another happy. Nor can he make another feel badly without using physical or emotionally abusive force. Sometimes the actions of one person are the focus of deep hurt and sadness in another. If the offender does not understand, or care, that another person struggles with his behavior, he will not feel badly about it. Therefore the offender has no reason to change his behavior. Again, the person who is hurting is the one that must change. The following is another illustration:

> *Joy and Tom are a married couple. During their first year of living together, Joy notices that Tom stops speaking with her when he is irritated and angry. When she asks him if he is irritated with her, he says, "No." However he will not elaborate on his answer or explain his mood. Joy does not know what to do to make things right again. As days go by without an explanation or a change in Tom, Joy begins to feel sad and detached. She does special favors for Tom and tries to stay out of his way, hoping his mood will improve. She asks repeatedly why he is angry. She apologizes for whatever "I did to make you so angry." Before the week's end, fatigued from walking on eggs, Joy is feeling depressed.*

This pattern of behavior repeats for several years before Joy learns how to resolve the problem. Even though Tom is the one that pulls away, Joy has to address what is causing her to feel hurt and not expect Tom to make a change.

Several important points in this vignette will guide the reader to an understanding of behavior change. Initially, Tom had a problem with something that Joy did. He chose to solve his problem by detaching from her and not talking with her. He projected responsibility for his feelings onto Joy or believed she was responsible for them. In turn, Tom's lack of communication created a problem for Joy. She believed she must have done something to irritate Tom. She felt badly without knowing what it was that she had done. At this point Joy is looking for Tom to change and Tom (believing he has done nothing wrong) is not responding to her hopes. He uses his silence to temporarily nurse his mood (unprocessed emotion) until he feels better. Once he feels better, he has no reason to change. Joy is at the mercy of Tom's mood and will not feel better until she can understand her part of the problem.

The solution: Joy has hurt feelings and is the one who owns the resulting problem. This is good because she now has the power to change the situation. Joy must realize what part of this dynamic is a problem for her. She does so by asking herself: *What about this situation is making me feel depressed?* Probably she would say that she does not like it when the two of them go several days without speaking. Most likely, she misses the closeness with Tom and the easy loving flow of their relationship. She hopes that Tom will change, but he is not changing his behavior. To change the situation, Joy must change her behavior.

With help from her therapist, Joy makes a personal reflection on her problem. She asks herself whether she is aware of anything she had said or done to Tom that is hurtful or mean. When she cannot think of anything, she agrees to stop apologizing for herself. Note, this does not mean that Joy does not participate in the problem, only that Tom has not told her why he is irritated. Next, she identifies the way she wants to be with Tom; she knows she does not want to stop talking to him. She promises herself that in the future she will continue to laugh and talk to him whether or not he responds. To be happy when he is irritated with her and shuts down feels foreign to her. She decides to speak to him in sentences that do not require a response. For instance: *I read something interesting online. It was about . . . . I left the Web link on the desk if you're interested* or *I've decided to run to the store and give you some quiet time, let me know if you would like anything.* When Joy decides not to take responsibility for Tom's irritation and not to participate in his mood, the negative dynamic that was so much a part of their relationship begins to subside. Within hours, Tom's mood dissipates and he is speaking and interacting with Joy as usual.

It can be difficult for a person to realize that she cannot change someone else's behavior. Even though one can readily observe when another is acting violently, foolishly, or pathetically, it is fruitless to expect or demand that the person change. Yet most of us try advising, cajoling, complaining, threatening, or bullying to get the other to change. In the end this can cause hard feelings and add further stress to the relationship, but it is rarely successful. It is difficult for most people to tell their story and then hear that, even though the behavior of the other is deplorable, the one who feels the hurt is the one who must change. He must be the one to change because he can change and because he wants to change. Consider the following:

> *A young mother of five children attends school part-time, trying to complete her college degree. She schedules her classes so she can be at home shortly after her children get home from school. For thirty minutes a day her teenage son is in charge. But she is faced with a daily dilemma: the kitchen is a mess. School bags are tossed on the counter, the refrigerator door is left open, snack fixings are strewn about, and the responsible child has not emptied the dishwasher. She complains repeatedly, asking the same questions:* Who left the peanut butter out? Who left the refrigerator door open? Why is the milk left on the table? *By the time the kitchen is cleaned up, she is irritated and short-tempered, which is not at all the way she wants to feel when she is with her children.*

This mom was not happy when I pointed out that she is the one—and not her children—who has a problem. She is the one who feels frustrated about the situation. Her children are feeling just fine about it and have no reason to change their behavior;

her comments to them had no effect. With a little direction, she was able to change her approach:

> *On Monday when she enters the kitchen, she quietly straightens the counter, empties the dishwasher, and cleans up spills from the floor and cabinets. She tells her children that this is the way she likes the kitchen to be when she starts dinner and that she has decided to change her behavior. She does not like feeling irritable and does not want to complain to them and raise her voice. Instead she explains to them that when the kitchen is in a mess, she will choose to not fix supper and go to the library to study instead. The children are pleased that she has accepted responsibility for the issue and go about their business.*
>
> *On Tuesday all is as usual. But when she enters her house, she greets each child and asks about their day. Then she tells them that she is on her way to the library to study and will be home in two hours. Little unbelieving faces look at her—isn't she going to fix supper? No, she explains, she does not enjoy working in a dirty kitchen. She is sure they will manage with the snacks that are available. Mom leaves for the library.*
>
> *On Wednesday, and most days after, she returns home to a kitchen in reasonably good condition. Although it is not perfect, she is grateful for her children's efforts. They have accepted responsibility for their mess and have made an obvious effort to change.*

The key to changing a situation by changing yourself is developing the ability to respond to others and to not overreact to the situation. Acting out one's irritation by yelling at or demeaning others is a low level of reactionary behavior that does not solve the problem. But choosing responsible behavior usually will.

Many problems are not so simple and involve carefully planned responses. For instance, when a person is living with an abusive spouse or is in a relationship with someone who might be dangerous, she must focus on her own behavior. She will never change the other, or the situation, by begging, threatening, or hoping the other will change. The responsibility to change must be on the one in physical or emotional pain. The one who is abused or endangered must be the one to leave and separate from the danger. The one who is abused must make a statement that is clear to the other: *I do not want to live like this. If you threaten me, hit me (or the children), or violate me in any way, I will leave you. I want you to seek help for your temper.*

If the other takes immediate positive action, there is some hope. However, the one that is abused must not take responsibility for making therapy appointments or reminding the other of his commitment. The one who is to change must take full responsibility. If and when there is no follow-through, the abused one must take the action and leave without further discussion. Most of the time, this level of change cannot happen without professional assistance and the support of family and friends. Counselors, safe houses, police protection, and attorneys play a significant role in assisting a victim, or potential victim, to change her situation. Yet she is the one that must change. She cannot afford to wait for the other to change.

The question: to change or not to change?

Beginning in infancy, human behavior is monitored and shaped by the expectations of others. First, parents, older siblings, and other family members encourage us toward behavior that fits in with that of the family. Proper behavior is learned and expected from family, neighbors, teachers, and society. As a part of the maturing process each person deviates from the expectations of others and tries new, personal ways of doing things. When this breaking out is encouraged and guided by responsible adults, a person learns to trust his decisions and develops his behavior style. Too often, though, people are afraid to develop an individual style and look to others to tell them what to do and how it should be done. Their behavior is chosen by what others want and what others expect from them.

Sometimes others might insist that you change your behavior. The healthy person must determine when or if he wants to change. Sometimes others insist that we act as they do and not in a way that is natural for us. Perhaps their suggestions do not take our gifts and talents into consideration. Perhaps they want us to act more like they think we should. Adolescence is a time when this dynamic is best expressed. Because it is the developmental task of a child to begin the process of separation from parents, it is more important to a ten- or twelve-year-old to be accepted by peers than by parents. It is most important to them that they dress like their friends, talk like their friends, and do as their friends do. They must express themselves individually as a part of their group while they avoid actions that would set them apart from peers. As an adolescent develops into an adult, this need for peer acceptance tempers itself and the person tends to choose behaviors based on personal experiences of success and achievement and positive feedback.

Not everyone easily makes the transition from pleasing their parents to pleasing themselves. Expectations of parents are preserved in memory and stay with us for years into adulthood. I have had clients in their fifties who say, *I can still hear my mother saying, why don't you act more like your sister?* or *Can't you do something with your hair—that style doesn't become you* or *Why do you want to study art? You'll never be able to earn a living.* Positive parental messages continue to strengthen self-esteem and sound more like: *You can do anything you set your mind to* or *Trust yourself—you are an intelligent person.* These early messages stay with us and play an important role in shaping our sense of who we are.

Most of us today have grown up with advertising messages and television commentators telling us how to look and act, what products to use, how to vote, and how to worship. Some of these messages are strong, predicting devastating consequences if the advice is not taken. Everyone is eventually faced with the questions: *What do I want?* and *Who do I want to be?* At some point we determine when or if we want to change to become who we want to be. We learn not to shape our behavior in response to the expectations of others.

It is difficult to change. First, a person must have some honest understanding of what she does that leaves others feeling friendly or annoyed. She must also identify which of her behaviors she likes. This is important, because an emotionally healthy person does not choose and gauge behavior merely by determining what others want her to be. Each person must identify what she most likes about herself, as well as what she would like to change. Then she must determine how to make the changes that she wants to make.

When working with clients, especially with women, I often ask: *How would you like it to be?* Invariably, she responds with something like: *Well, I don't want him to do that anymore or I don't want my daughter to talk back to me.* I remind the client that the actual question is: *How would you like it to be?* not *What don't you like?* Many people have a difficult time identifying what it is that they need and want. It is so much easier to complain about what they don't want. When asked what they do want, they need time to think about the question because their answer will affect the way in which they respond. For example, Jenny, a mother of three teenage daughters, yells at them: *I hate the screaming and arguing that goes on in this family. Everyone is rude and thoughtless. I am sick and tired of it!*

This statement might invite screaming and argumentative responses, or no response from her daughters. Or Jenny might have stated what she does want followed by a statement of the behavior she plans to start using herself: *I really want our home to be more peaceful and less chaotic. One thing I am going to start doing is to talk in a quieter manner. I'm going to try to stop yelling and use a kinder tone. You may want to listen more carefully. If you miss what I have to say, you will have to take the consequences. I am no longer going to nag you.* Speaking in a quiet tone, Jenny is explaining what she wants and how she intends to change the situation by changing her own behavior.

It is a temptation to pay more attention to another's behavior than to our own. Common practice is for someone to observe others and make mental notes about what they do and how they do it. The observer then compares what he sees to his own behavior and judges whether it is right or acceptable. It is difficult for someone to hear a point of view or experience that does not complement or support his own view. Without self-reflection, people generally do not know themselves very well. A person can control her behavior when she can observe her actions and make an honest assessment of herself. A good place to start is to make a list with two columns: 1) *What do I like about myself* and 2) *What about myself would I like to change.* This can be an ongoing exercise, with continuing self-reflection.

Points to remember about behavior change:

- Reaction does not engage a cognitive process and is a primitive form of behavior.
- Response engages a cognitive process of reason and is a higher form of behavior.
- If you are the one who feels badly, you must own the problem and are the only one who can resolve it.
- You cannot change another's behavior—you can only change your own.
- You do not have the power to make another person happy—or to make another person angry.
- Someone else is not responsible for your happiness—or your pain (unless you are controlled by physical or psychological abuse and cannot get away from your abuser).
- You can only change a situation by changing yourself.
- When you cannot change the situation and the other cannot or will not change, the only way to change the situation is to separate from it.
- When the behavior of the other is dangerous, professional support may be necessary to separate.

Chapter 3

When the Other Cannot Change

If you don't like something, change it; if you can't change it, change the way you think about it.

Mary Engelbreit, American artist

Brain disorders

According to psychiatrist James Whitney Hicks, nearly half of us have a family member or close friend who suffers from a serious mental illness. In 2001, approximately 15 million adults age eighteen or older were estimated to have suffered from a serious mental illness during the past year. Less than half of these people received treatment. In my experience, most individuals that I have seen in therapy have encountered some kind of mental illness in their extended family. It may be an affective disorder, like depression or anxiety; addiction to alcohol or chemicals; or a more serious condition, like bipolar disorder or schizophrenia.

In the past, brain disease was commonly referred to as *mental* illness. However, this label is restrictive and misleading, since some brain disorders do not limit the mental process, while mental dysfunction is due to brain disorder. Brain disorders, or central nervous system disorders, produce symptoms like mood swings, lack of empathy, lack of caring, and uncontrolled emotions that affect impulse control and attention, as well as mental processes.

When there is an untreated disease or disorder in the brain, a person's ability to choose behavior can be impaired. Because he may not be able to reason and make a rational choice about his behavior, he may be incapable of responding. Instead, this person is more likely to react to imagined or real stimuli. One of the symptoms of brain disease is a pattern of frequent, long-lasting, and intense inappropriate behavior. Such behavior is a part of the human condition—everyone acts inappropriately or exhibits odd behavior at times. Much of our humor stems from the ability to laugh at common mistakes and our bizarre reactions to life situations. However, when a person's behavior is more bizarre than what most people consider to be normal, or he thinks or acts irrationally more often than not, and the behavior lasts for days, weeks, or months, he may suffer from a brain disorder. Personality disorders fit into this category and manifest in many ways and with various degrees of severity.

Without professional and medical attention, the affected person may not be able to control his emotions or behavior and cannot be expected to change. Therefore, it is imperative for family members to learn how to modify their own behavior in order to cultivate stability in their lives, while maintaining a workable relationship with the person suffering from the disorder.

Life with someone with a brain disorder can be extremely challenging, yet it can also be manageable. The key lies in the ability of family and friends to learn about the illness and help the patient cope with and manage the disease. Generally, families do best when they enter into the therapeutic process to learn a behavior style that will be of assistance to them. Again, it is difficult for family and friends to understand that they are the ones that must change because they can change. Change in the family or environment is affected when the ones that can change do change. Their change in behavior can create a stable environment where the unstable member can function at his best, and the stress of friends and family is kept at a minimum. This is illustrated best by the work of organizations like AL-ANON, which has a membership that consists of the family and friends of alcoholics, and the National Alliance for the Mentally Ill (NAMI), which is a national organization whose members support and assist others who suffer from disorders of the brain. Both organizations encourage family and friends of the one affected to educate themselves about the disorder, learn healthy behaviors, and encourage their loved one to stay in treatment for his illness.

The focus of these programs is to teach families and friends to learn skills to separate themselves from the emotional ups and downs of their loved ones, change their expectations of the ill one, and learn to reduce their own stress. This can create a stable environment where everyone can function at their best. One woman shared that at one time she felt that she was riding a roller coaster with her husband's emotional illness. After therapy, she now stays on the ground and waits for him until his "ride" is over. Many organizations and community service groups exist to assist caregivers in this difficult, but rewarding, personal journey.

Sociopathic behavior

Sociopathic behavior is described in the *Diagnostic and Statistical Manual of Mental Disorders* (published by the American Psychiatric Association) as Antisocial Personality Disorder. Yet to some this label is so broad that it negates the significance and seriousness of this illness. When a person with this disorder is evaluated and charged with a crime, he may be referred to as a *psychopath*. The terms *sociopath* and *psychopath* are often used interchangeably. I prefer the term *sociopath* because I use it in my discussions of relationships in everyday life. I will also use the pronoun "he" since, according to neuropsychology researcher Kent Kiehl, sociopathy is most often found in men. In a 2010 issue of *Scientific American Mind,* Kiehl writes:

> People with the disorder make up 0.5 to 1 percent of the general population. When you discount children, women (for reasons that remain a puzzle, few women are afflicted), and those who are already incarcerated, that translates to approximately 250,000 psychopaths living freely in the U.S.

As research continues to unveil the nature of this disease, its definition and methods of treatment will surely become clearer. Dr. Kiehl has studied the brain scans of hundreds of prisoners at the Western New Mexico Correctional Facility. He theorizes that psychopathy, or generalized pathology, corresponds to a deficit in the paralimbic region of the brain. Sociopathy, or pathology that endangers others, occurs when there is a malfunction in the ability of the midbrain to relay emotional information to the cortex.

Although a sociopath understands the word that names a feeling or emotion, he is unable to process the emotional feeling associated with the word. For example, he may know it is wrong to hit a child, but he does not feel badly when he does it. Thus the sociopath does not have the ability to associate a feeling with his actions. Nor can a sociopath understand or know what another feels; he cannot relate or connect to another person emotionally. A sociopath lacks the capacity for empathy or compassion. To the sociopath, others are only an extension of his pleasure or pain. Such a person does not have the ability to make a moral decision about the way his behavior affects the lives of those around him. As a result, even though the sociopath knows at some level that a behavior is wrong, or even criminal, he cannot see how an action is connected to himself or to another person. He adapts what American psychiatrist Hervey Cleckley calls a "mask of sanity." He covers his lack of caring with a superficial, but convincing, mask of politeness and charm, even consideration. For instance:

> *Jim appears to have a wonderful, thoughtful personality. On a first date with Irene he is more polite and generous than other men she has dated. He is quick to open the car door for her, he lightly touches her elbow as he guides her across a street, he pulls out her chair at dinner, and he kisses her gently on the cheek. Onlookers are impressed with his cool demeanor. Later, when they order, he is quick to suggest the right entrée for Irene and chooses the perfect wine. Irene is quite impressed. After a month or two of this wonderful treatment, she is sure she has met the man of her dreams.*
>
> *One night Irene decides she wants to choose her own entrée at dinner and, seeing a male friend in the restaurant, she exchanges a hug and friendly words with him. She is surprised when Jim reacts angrily and seems irritated during the rest of the evening. After they arrive at her home, he begins to ridicule, insult, and mock her. Irene challenges his mistreatment of her. An argument ensues and escalates until Jim hits Irene and knocks her against a wall. Irene is shocked and wonders what she did to cause his anger.*

Sociopathic behavior takes many shapes and forms. Yet the basic form does not change that much. In the above example, Jim's behavior has nothing to do with Irene. Jim does not have the capacity to care about her, all of his actions are about him. His courteous demeanor is a show for those around him. His aim is to evoke responses from observers: *Look at Jim, isn't he a wonderful guy? She is so lucky to be with him. I would love to find someone like him.*

Irene feels good about the way Jim is treating her. But Jim has no real awareness about how Irene feels. He is playing a role.

Comments and compliments are memorized behaviors that have nothing to do with her. He has no capacity for empathy. After dinner, he makes no connection between the feelings generated during this dinner and feelings from previous dates. He is only aware that Irene's behavior, independent of his planning and control, generates anger and rage in him. He is enraged by her words with her friend and does not understand why she would pay attention to anyone but him. His attention is directed only to himself and the relationship is only about him.

Irene is merely a prop that enhances Jim's performance. When another person steps into his scene, he is filled with rage. He reacts to this with strong emotion and is completely unconcerned about how it affects Irene. He is the only player in his drama. All of his decisions and actions have one goal, which is to make him think he is powerful and in control. When she makes a decision for herself, independent of him, and includes someone else for only a few minutes, he is threatened. He reacts to this threat with rage and destructive behavior.

A sociopath functions in his environment by controlling it. To have control, he must also control the lives of those around him. He controls others by manipulating the environment where others live, work, play, worship, or participate in society. The sociopath finds a place in society, not by making emotional connections to others, but by playing a role that charms others and draws them into his manipulative pattern. A familiar story is that of the charming suitor who is attracted to and eventually marries an elderly woman. He then empties her bank accounts, leaves her, changes his name, and finds his next prey. The behaviors he uses to manipulate and impress others are memorized and after a time can be recognized as a pattern. The sociopath is not spontaneous—his destructive behavior is cold and calculated. Yet his reaction to change or loss of control can be impulsive and dangerous. He can-

Sociopathic Behavior

Sociopathic behavior is very difficult to identify in a therapy session. Unless it is blatant, it may take many sessions to recognize that a client is a sociopath. The person's slick manner might be about charming the therapist in order to gain control and manipulate the focus of the therapy. He might be ready with compliments and sometimes even gifts. The therapist can test his sincerity by gently refusing his attention. Remember that he is vulnerable when he thinks someone is on to him, and with these refusals he will begin to get irritated.

If the therapist accelerates her challenges he will probably stop coming to therapy, or he might become unpredictable and dangerous. The therapist must expect this in order to avoid putting herself and her client in danger. In any case, it can be extremely dangerous to confront a sociopath. The clinician must use some form of manipulation to regain control. A telephone at hand for immediate assistance is essential. In places I have worked, clinicians agree on a signal or a loud noise that will alert others to come immediately into the room. In some therapy clinics it is common to have very small windows above the knobs of the doors to the consulting rooms. This signals to a client that others are going about their business on the other side of the door and are aware that a therapy session is taking place. Some clinics have alarms in the rooms. Once the sociopathic person is identified, the therapist must discontinue therapy with this person. This presents another danger—to reject a sociopath can make him defensive and dangerous.

I was confronted with this type of situation about twenty years ago before I had any real knowledge or experience at identifying sociopathic behavior. I met with a husband and wife alone for one session of marital therapy. The husband, insisting that he wanted to become a better person, asked for several individual sessions. I soon realized that his only aim was to sway me to his side. I felt increasingly uncomfortable with him but afraid to stop the individual sessions. A colleague instructed me to get him to fire me. *What?* I asked, having no idea what he meant. He explained that the sociopath cannot tolerate a situation unless he can control it. My colleague suggested that I call him the morning of his session and tell him I needed to reschedule. Although quite irritated, the client agreed to the change. Before the rescheduled session, I called him again. This time I said I was running late and would have to see him late afternoon instead of the usual 10 a.m. He became enraged: *What kind of a therapist are you? I don't have time for this. . . .* I never saw this man again.

not control his impulses for long. Instead, his anger builds until he seems to explode in verbal and/or physical violence.

A sociopath does not come to therapy unless he is threatened by a life-altering change that he cannot control such as divorce, loss of employment, or loss of child visitation or custody. When he does come for counseling, his motive is to regain control. He is a smooth talker and his goal is to deceive the therapist and gain support against the threat he perceives. He is not there to change his behavior; he is there to get the therapist to agree with him and side against his partner or to fulfill a mandate of the court. When he cannot get the therapist's support for his side, he discontinues therapy, blaming the therapist or his wife for *not knowing what she is talking about* or for *taking his spouse's side and ganging up on him.*

The sociopath is a pathological liar. To him truth and illusion are all the same. He will tell a story so ably that it will seem plausible to those around him. Even if the story is proven to be false, he will maintain his position.

Because manipulation is his method of functioning, the sociopath is a master of disguise. His goal in life is to look good to those around him. He is often physically attractive and has a practiced charm that seduces others into clamoring for his attention and friendship. The sociopath is the proverbial Dr. Jekyll and Mr. Hyde. The face he presents to the public is charming, caring, and attractive. However, in his private life he can be cold, cruel, and devoid of empathy and caring toward others. He will do everything he possibly can to protect his public image and hide his private reality.

When someone meets or interacts with a sociopath, she often comments, *I can't believe he did that* or *How can anyone be so mean?* Sociopaths take pleasure in the suffering of others. One fraternity brother took great pride in his reputation for hitting pledges so hard with a paddle that it knocked them off their feet, causing them to writhe in pain on the floor. He flaunted his reputation as a cruel pledge master and equated violence with manliness.

Sociopaths cannot tolerate confrontation. When they meet someone who does not buy into their manipulative schemes, they become outrageously mean. They will do something to hurt the other to show their control of him. It is not unusual for a sociopath to scheme against anyone who stands in the way of a job promotion. He will find a way to ruin the reputation of anyone who he believes overshadows him. Because he is delusional and passive-aggressive, he will often attack another emotionally without the other ever knowing who it was that hurt her or what triggered the behavior. The sociopath will take pride and pleasure in making another suffer and, in the end, blame his victim for some imagined offense.

The sociopath's idea of humor and fun is to make a spectacle of someone else. He will deride and chide in a hurtful way, although he is not one to laugh at himself. If he is the target of laughter and fun, he will take it personally and seek revenge. No one will get away with laughing at him.

According to recent research, sociopathy is both a genetic condition and a result of environmental exposure. The degree of the disturbance may depend on whether an individual has the genetic disposition or has been raised in an environment controlled by a sociopathic parent or caregiver. Sometimes, when the behavior is learned in a sociopathic environment, the one suffering from the condition can make change with treatment. On the other hand, if one has the genetic disposition but is raised in a loving and caring environment, the condition might not develop into a disorder. But when both genetic and environmental influences are present, research does not show a good prognosis for change. Sociopaths cannot participate in a healthy relationship and are generally dangerous to others. They are often responsible for physical harm that manifests as domestic violence, leading to emotionally battered spouses and abused children and elderly family members.

Sociopaths are masters in abuse that leaves no physical sign. They heap psychological abuse and neglect on partners and children and too often cover up their behavior with their charming public mask. Their behavior usually goes unnoticed by outsiders until a family member suffers a serious physical injury or is killed. The constant abuse that leaves no visible scars goes unnoticed and is usually witnessed only by those who live or work with the sociopath. It is not uncommon for the partner of a sociopath to take the blame for his behavior. In *The Sociopath Next Door,* Martha Stout estimates that sociopaths constitute 25 percent of the population.

Whether or not one agrees with Stout, most will agree that too many people are affected by a parent, spouse, or life partner who bullies and manipulates those around them to get what he wants. Generally, victims of sociopaths hold out hope for years that he will change. Spouses are afraid to leave and children grow up trying to stay out of his way or denying that he is abusive. The facts, however, show that the sociopath can be found living in seemingly ordinary homes, coaching sports, teaching in schools, and at our sides as co-workers. He can be our landlord, our attorney, our medical doctor, or our therapist. We have all known them as priests, nuns, neighbors, and police officers. They often wield great influence in our politics, our religion, and our military.

This personality disorder, which so strongly features the need to control and exert authority over others, when combined with alcohol and drugs, can be lethal. One should never expect him to change. He is dangerous. Get away from him.

It would be biased and unfair here not to mention the role of the sociopathic woman. She is present in our lives as well. I most often see her in my practice as a mother and wife. She is the woman who gets married for prestige. Fulfillment and gratification come for her from sharing in the possessions or status of her husband or from being a mother or just from the mere fact of being married. The love and attention she directs toward her husband is a mask and, once she is settled in, she finds him to be an annoyance or of no real use to her. She appears to her co-workers, her children's teachers, fellow church members, and other mothers to be the ideal mother and wife. She may look good in public, but at home she is a monster.

This ideal woman berates her husband and children and controls every part of their lives. She quickly destroys outside relationships and, although she might surround herself with people, she has no real friends. She only allows people to get close if they are useful to her. And she does not tolerate her husband's friends or family, because her need to control is threatened by outsid-

Characteristics of a Sociopath

Since every person's behavior is unique, no one person will exhibit all of these characteristics. This list draws on the sources listed at the end of this book as well as symptoms that I have observed in my work:

- Sociopaths have a superficial charm that masks a dominating and mean personality. It is more important for them to look good rather than to be good. They often surround themselves with people who adore them and are willing to follow their lead without questioning or confronting them.
- Sociopaths are pathological liars. Exceptionally convincing, they will swear to the lie even after proven wrong. Because their lies are delusions, they believe them to be true and can pass a lie-detector test. Often their whole life appears to be a lie masked by their leadership in a religion, a profession, or a nonprofit group that gives them a self-image of benevolence and control. They are not identified until their behavior is confronted by someone stronger than they are, such as a law enforcement officer. Even after they are found out, some acquaintances will not believe the charges leveled against the sociopath.
- Sociopaths can show outrage about insignificant events but remain unmoved by tragic ones. They cannot relate or empathize with the feelings or needs of others. Their emotions are shallow, and they alternate between displaying superficial emotion and outrage. They put on a good show for others.
- Sociopaths exhibit impulsive and risky behaviors. They might be involved with some criminal activity such as tax evasion, fighting, driving under the influence, petty

theft, or insurance fraud. They do not think what they do is wrong and have no concern about the effect on their victims. Instead, they consider their crime to have been taking advantage of an opportunity.

- Sociopaths are mean-spirited. Quick to use physical punishment and humiliate others, they are indifferent to the pain and misery they cause others. In fact, they relish and enjoy pulling something over on another. They frequently engage in activities such as promiscuity, pornography, and gambling. Because of their controlling and mean behavior, sociopaths do not maintain long-term friendships, employment, or intimate relationships.
- Sociopaths typically make terrible parents because they dehumanize their children, using them to enhance their fantasies about themselves. They may belittle, mock, and visit emotional abuse on their children. And they do not see harm in physical or sexual abuse of children. Physical and emotional bullies, they model sociopathic behavior to their children.
- Sociopaths often appear to be popular because they surround themselves with people who adore them or are entranced by their charm. Yet they make life hell for those close to them and control them by withholding attention or instilling fear of violence and abandonment. Those who see through their superficial charm or have experienced their violence feel like they are walking on eggs in their presence.
- Sociopaths have a grandiose view of themselves. They see themselves as all-knowing and all-powerful and better than others. Believing they have an inherent right to be respected and honored, they do not, however, respect and honor others unless it allows them to make an impression.
- Sociopaths do not apologize with sincerity and do not

feel shame, guilt, or remorse. They will make superficial amends until they are sure they are again looking good and regaining the confidence of their victims. They choose partners who are vulnerable and likely to become dependent on them.

- Sociopaths enjoy violence and entertainment that is violent. They are attracted to film and music that depict physical or emotional suffering.
- Sociopaths are irresponsible and evade the consequences of their behavior. They often look for someone to take care of them. They will maintain a long-term relationship if they can use that relationship to get their needs met, especially if they are not expected to give anything back.

ers. After a couple of years, her spouse realizes that he has lost contact with his friends and rarely sees his family. He is isolated in her controlled environment. She displays no empathy or compassion for her family's concerns or hurts, neglecting the emotional needs of her children and spending most of her time entertaining herself.

The sociopathic woman does not create a nurturing environment, often leaving her house disorganized or filthy. Or, if her house is where she shines, it might be a showplace for others. Her emphasis is not on making a home for her family; rather, it is on how her house reflects her. She will put this same emphasis on her children. Their looks, performances, and personalities must bring pride to her; not because she is proud of her children, but because they are only an extension of her. If she has a career, she might make a habit of leaving her children in day care for hours after the scheduled pick-up time, so that she can spend time with friends or go to a bar.

When I first began my practice in the 1980s, most of us associated domestic violence and child abuse with men. When police were involved with a domestic complaint, the husband spent the night in jail. It took some time to realize that husbands are not necessarily or always the culprits. Yet that bias still prevails. I have counseled many couples where the wife was just plain mean, regularly attacking her husband with knives or other objects. Such a wife can hit, kick, scream, and yell as well as any man. She locks him out of the house and sells his possessions without his knowledge. But if he calls 911, it is sometimes impossible to convince the officer that the *pretty little thing* is vicious and her six-foot-tall husband is a victim. If he fights back against her abuse, she will accuse him of violence and, most of the time, her story will be believed.

When her selfish and often-expensive ways begin to destroy her marriage, she lets her husband know that if he leaves her he will never see his children again. And she knows she is capable of this. She will construct any lie to demean him and make him look bad in court. She will accuse him of child abuse and might even throw herself against a sharp table or other object to make bruises that she will photograph and present in court. She will call 911 and file a personal protective order against him, accusing him of being dangerous. There is no end to what she will do to destroy both him and his relationship with his children. The sad truth is that she does not care about the children. They are only props to make her look good and help her to get spousal and child support that she has no intention of spending on the children. She will ruin her children's lives to rid herself of a husband she has come to see as a nuisance.

Although this scenario can just as well describe the sociopathic behavior of a man, it is very common in women. When married to a sociopathic woman, a man must find a way to get out of the relationship. Again, the only way to change the relationship is to get away from it. In order for him to do this, he will need the counsel of a good attorney and a family therapist, and he must document her behavior.

Points to remember about brain disorders:

- Mental illness is better referred to as brain disease or brain disorder, because all diseases of the brain do not cause impairment of mental functioning.
- When someone has an untreated brain disease or disorder, his ability to choose behavior can be impaired.
- When a person's behavior is more bizarre than what most people consider normal, or that person thinks or acts irrationally more often than not, and the behavior lasts for days, weeks, or months, she may suffer from a brain disorder.
- Without professional and/or medical attention, a person with a brain disorder may not be able to control her emotions or behavior and cannot be expected to change.
- Family members and friends do best when they enter into the therapeutic process to learn a behavior style that will assist them.
- Change in the family or environment is affected when the ones that can change succeed in doing so.
- Family members must learn to separate themselves from the emotional ups and downs of their loved ones with a brain disorder. They must change their expectations of the one that is ill and learn to reduce their own stress, creating a stable environment where everyone can function at their best.

- Sociopaths do not seek therapy unless they want to gain control of another person. They use their time to convince the therapist that they are right and the other is wrong.
- True sociopaths do not change their behavior.

Chapter 4

Know Yourself

He who knows others is wise. He who knows himself is enlightened.

Lao Tzu, Chinese philosopher

Who are you?

Many people find it uncomfortable to focus on themselves. Our training urges us to be aware of others and to do good things for them, putting their needs and comfort before our own. The value of this is undisputed; however, we cannot consider others to the exclusion of ourselves. To think of yourself first is not an act of selfishness. A Christian mandate that guides many people today is to love God, above all, and love your neighbor as yourself. The Golden Rule, *Do to others as you would have them do to you,* can be traced back to the days of Confucius. This dictum presumes that you treat yourself well, and this is not selfishness. In order to give yourself to another, you must have something to give. It is essential that you nurture, educate, pamper, and take care of yourself.

A healthy, well-balanced, pleasant person has much to offer to others. Yet, it seems to me that a hurting, angry, resentful person might use and manipulate others in order to feel better about himself. His behavior is energy-draining and, ultimately, can do more harm than good. Great spiritual leaders spend time in prayer, reflection, eating, singing, dancing, and having fun with friends. They increase their energy to have a plentiful source to share in the form of love and service to others. It is very difficult to be there for another when you are emotionally depleted.

To take good care of yourself, it is essential that you know yourself. You must know your needs and determine what is good for you. A good way to begin this discovery is to write your story. Begin with your childhood memories and see how they relate to what you know about yourself today. Begin writing without regard to grammar and form. Try to write for yourself, as if nobody will ever read what you write. This way, your thoughts can be a vehicle for you to focus on your view of yourself. Knowing that nobody will read your self-reflection will allow you the freedom to be candid and honest. If there is a chance that a housemate or a family member might find and read your writing, consider using

Guidelines for Reflection on Your Story

Here are several questions that will help you begin the process of getting to know yourself. You might find it helpful to write a paragraph or a few pages about each of these:

- When and where were you born? What was happening around you?
- Who are your parents and grandparents, great-grandparents?
- What is their story and how has it affected your life?
- Given what you know, what kind of people do you think they may have been?
- What traits do you think you might share with them?
- Can you identify the gifts and talents of these people?
- What were their specific life challenges?
- How are you like or not like them?

- What is your earliest memory?
- How did you think of yourself as a child?
- How does your childhood affect who you are today?
- Are your childhood memories verifiable? Children can be confused about the difference between memories, fantasies, and what others have told them.
- Who were your best friends?
- Why were you drawn to these people?
- If you could do or be anything you wanted, and money was not a problem, what would you do or be?
- How would this change benefit you?
- Where do you look for happiness?
- How do you interact with others?
- What kind of friends do you attract?
- With whom do you feel most comfortable?

code words, shorthand, or create a password-protected document. Record what comes to you as you reflect on your life. This is not an exercise for one sitting. Rather, it may lead to a continuing journal that will reveal your approach to spirituality and your insights and patterns of behavior. You will be able to identify what activities and environments help you feel balanced and at peace, as well as those that cause stress and affect you in a negative way.

Once you have begun to write the story of you, find someone with whom you can share your insights in an accepting and confidential setting. Seek out a person who genuinely cares about you—a therapist, a spiritual director, or a supportive friend. Often trusting friends can do these exercises together in small groups or pairs. We tend to grow more consciously when we have a *truth-speaker* who will give us honest and wholesome feedback in a caring manner. When seeking out a person with whom to share, find someone who is working to improve her own life. Look for someone who understands your lifestyle and life choices. Often people seek out a pastor or parish priest only because they are available, even though this person's lifestyle may be quite different from their own.

It is better to choose a guide other than your life partner or spouse. Good relationships can be strained when a spouse is allowed to become a therapist or personal guide. Because your partner's life is so much a part of your experience, his observations about you are more subjective and can be blurred by his emotions or hopes and fears for you. Your partner has a significant emotional investment in you.

It works best when you can share your insights and new self-awareness with your spouse once you better understand them yourself and are ready. The reverse of this is also true: your life partner will not appreciate you as a therapist. Your spouse or partner, like you, deserves his own therapeutic and spiritual companion. It has been my experience that it is an imposition when one partner is expected to follow the same emotional or spiritual path as the other. Even though you might share the same religion or philosophies, your manner of expression will be different. You might differ in your choice of spiritual readings and place of worship.

It is not uncommon for people to find themselves working with a therapist who will accept their medical insurance payment, rather than the one who is the best fit for them. Interview the person you are considering. Be assertive in your questions. Ask yourself whether you can trust and respect this person. Ask her to tell you some of her story, since it is important that she has walked a similar journey. Sometimes gender is an important consideration. Often women do better talking with women and men with men. However, this is not always true—the reverse may be a better choice for you. If you are not completely confident in your choice, or if at some point you lose confidence, find someone else.

Another important way to get to know yourself is to understand your personality. When you discover how you experience life, how you process information, and how you choose behaviors, your understanding of yourself will expand. There are many personality inventories and a plethora of fun quizzes forwarded in hundreds of e-mails and printed in the Sunday newspapers. These all tell you something about yourself. Generally, however, they are not valid or reliable and are designed for fun or to promote advertising. But they can help you question how you respond to your environment and give you a little information about yourself. You will, in my opinion, do better with an inventory that has proven reliable and helpful. I prefer the personality theory of Carl G. Jung because it is interesting and fun. Everyone enjoys learning about themselves, especially when that information is accurate and painless.

A brief overview of Carl G. Jung's personality theory

Jung identified sixteen basic personalities. Because variations of personality are infinite, your personality is as different from others as are your fingerprints. A criticism of Jung's theory is that his personality indicators tend to label people, limiting their view of themselves and their potential. Yet this is no truer than recognizing that Jeanie is labeled because she has brown eyes and is different from her friend Sally, whose eyes are blue. Brown and blue are identifiers for physical traits, with countless variations for each. Jung's theory offers similar identifiers for psychological traits—with an infinite number of variations in every personality. Each of us is as unique in our personality as we are in our physical body.

According to Jung, opposites do attract. It is common for a person to believe she is attracted to a best friend or a life partner because *We have so much in common.* In truth, people's attractions to others are often based on their different ways of experiencing what they have in common. It is exciting to see in another those qualities and traits that we do not recognize, or have not developed, in ourselves. When a person is with someone who has some opposite personality traits, he feels whole or more complete because each compensates for the other's personality gaps or undeveloped traits. A sign of a good friendship is when someone says to his friend: *I feel so good about me when I'm with you.*

Being with the other or opposite, serves as a catalyst for a person to continue to develop her personality. For example, if Mary is fun-loving, outgoing, and friendly, Joan, who is quiet and reserved, will find her exciting and fun. Joan's own fun-loving spirit will come alive when she is with Mary. At the same time, Mary will appreciate Joan's company and her quiet, peaceful manner. Each will complement the other. Over the course of their friendship, each will develop further her opposite traits and feel more comfortable with herself. This is one explanation for the way in which life partners are attracted to one another and, over a period of time, develop similar personalities.

In couples, this dynamic of attraction can become a dynamic of dissension because it forces us to mature in ways we do not anticipate. Because we wrongly assume that the other is just like us, we expect him to want what we want and to act as we do. But the opposite is often true. The other's personality traits are not the same as ours and, because we have opposite traits, the other will often behave exactly opposite from what we expect. These personality differences cause conflict in a relationship until we understand what is happening. Personality differences are usually an easy fix in couples therapy, but when they go unidentified they are a common cause of dissatisfaction and resentment and can even lead to a break-up. Pete and Sue give us a good example:

Pete works for a large company. At a minimum of ten hours, his days are long. His job is close to home and he is usually home in fifteen minutes. When Pete arrives home every day, he quietly goes to the sofa, turns on the TV, and zones out. He does not seem to enjoy listening to Sue talk about her day. She continues to talk to him from the kitchen, where she is preparing supper. Sue asks Pete what he wants to eat, but he does not answer her. She tells him about the school open house, and he does not comment. She begins to recite the details of her day, their children's activities, and the neighborhood news. Pete not only does not respond, he becomes visibly annoyed by her monologue. He tries to concentrate on the TV show he is watching but has lost track of the program. Feeling exhausted, he now turns to the computer. Sue becomes furious, telling Pete that he is selfish and detached. She accuses him of not caring about the family. Pete protests and leaves the room. Sue follows, shouting that he never wants to talk and always walks away when she is talking to him. Both avoid each other for the rest of the evening. Sue calls her mother and talks about how unhappy she is.

Believe it or not, this is a scene that happens regularly in many households. Why is it so common? First, Pete identifies himself as an introvert, one who processes, or thinks about, information subjectively or internally. He is a good worker and gets along well with his co-workers. After expending energy all day and talking with many people, his fifteen-minute drive home does not provide him with enough quiet time to process his day and recoup his energy. Sue is a stay-at-home mom who has spent all day interacting with children and neighbors. She, too, is drained but for different reasons than Pete. During her busy day she hasn't had anyone to talk to about it. She is anxious to talk with Pete about her day.

Sue has an extroverted personality and processes information objectively, or externally, preferably by talking. She needs to talk and Pete lacks the energy to listen or take in her information. Both Pete and Sue are acting in ways that are normal. Neither of them is doing anything wrong, but each can do better if they learn to identify their own personality traits and emotional needs and those of their partners. Each must make adjustments if their individual needs are to be met. For example, Pete needs some wind-down time and Sue needs some wind-up time. Note that from the perspective of me, the therapist, this is an easy fix, but change will probably not happen if the problem is not identified. After making an effort to understand Sue's point of view, Pete will come in the door and greet Sue affectionately and then go upstairs to change his clothes. Sue will hold back her conversation until Pete returns. He will spend about twenty minutes changing, putting his clothes away, and being alone with thoughts. This time, along with the fifteen-minute drive, will allow him the time to recoup his energy. Then it will be his responsibility to go back to his wife and initiate a conversation. He will ask about her day, listen to what she has to say, and talk with her.

So far, both Sue and Pete are asking each other to do something uncomfortable—Sue must be quiet when she is bursting with conversation and Pete must talk when he prefers to be silent. While Sue is talking, she can be confident that Pete will not interrupt her. She must learn to pace her conversation, giving him time to take the information in, process it, and respond. If she continues talking without a pause, Pete might stop listening—not because he doesn't care, but because he must emotionally digest what he has taken in. She will do best if she invites a response and is quiet while Pete thinks before he responds. Pete will not be able to respond as she hopes if he must respond immediately without thinking. He might need thirty seconds or a week, depending on the seriousness of the situation.

When one partner demands an immediate response, the other might shut down, often leaving the room. It will work better if the one who is more extroverted announces what she wants to talk about and invites her partner to think about it: *I want to tell you about the meeting I had with Jack's teacher. She thinks he needs more help at home. I told her I would call her on Wednesday. Can we discuss this tonight?* Now the extrovert must be quiet and the introvert must respond, suggesting a time when he can pay full attention to the topic.

This example shows only one aspect of personality. Further reading will assist you in learning additional "easy" fixes that can balance and enhance your relationships. I recommend that you check the sources listed at the end of this book for a more in-depth discussion of Jung's personality theory.

Personal shadow

The shadow is a psychological term first introduced by Jung, and it defines the opposite characteristics of the ego. Whereas the ego represents everything about you that is conscious, or known to you, the shadow holds everything about you that is unconscious. Everything about you that you have repressed or denied or have never been aware of is a part of your shadow. Although you are unaware of your shadow's characteristics, they are often noticeable to others. Others have a different view of you than you have of yourself. You cannot realistically know yourself unless you are willing to look at your shadow self and bring these qualities, both negative and positive, to awareness.

If you have a hint that something about you is unacceptable, you may close your mind and deny it, pushing it to the dark corridors of your unconscious. The same is often true of your most awesome personal characteristics. Sometimes we are unable to admit to ourselves that we are awesome. Rather than own or accept these bad and good traits, you project them into the environment, unconsciously assigning them to others.

Earlier I explained undeveloped personality traits. These are also a part of our shadow. You recognize good stories, films, and art because you can place yourself in the films and relate to the stories and characters. This projection allows you to relate to the story, as though you are one of the characters. Not only do you see your conscious self in the drama, but the story can reveal your shadow self when you have an emotional reaction to one of the characters. For instance, you might hate the villain because the villain is playing out characteristics that you have but would not like to admit to. Or maybe the villain is acting out something that you have thought about doing, and you know you are capable of it. But you have never done it and wouldn't consciously consider it. Or you align yourself with the hero or heroine because within you there is a hero or a heroine, even though you might not consciously recognize it or you are afraid to act in a heroic manner.

You also project your shadow traits onto other people. As explained earlier, when you make a friend, you might feel intimidated or threatened because she is more educated or more attractive than you. You might think you do not like her because she thinks that she is better than everyone else. But, in fact, you don't like her because being with her reminds you that you are not happy with your level of education or you have not developed the ability to realize your own beauty. Instead of owning your disappointment in yourself, you feel conflict with the other. When you can identify this shadow quality, you will be able to realize that education is only one facet of an individual and does not indicate worth. You will no longer have the conflict when you realize that you too are an intelligent person and are capable of learning in other ways. Or, perhaps you will realize that you are not as educated, or as intelligent, as the other and can accept this fact and realize that your self-worth is not affected one way or another. You make enemies in the same way, unconsciously assigning your unrecognized traits onto others and then being repulsed by these same traits

Even though you are not aware of it, your shadow has a great influence on the way you interact with others and your environment. I explain to clients that the shadow can be like the blind spot when we are driving. Just because you are unaware of the vehicle next to you does not mean it is not there. To be safe, you must use a mirror and look to the right or left. How many times have you asked someone if your clothing is hanging straight? We do this because we cannot see parts of ourselves without the assistance of someone else, and other people are like mirrors to us. We project our image of ourselves onto the mirror before we can see what is in it. In the same way, we project our shadow image onto others and then see that image in them. Let's look at the following examples:

> *Jean is well liked by her friends. She has a circle of women that she regularly meets with for dinner. One evening, a new woman, Jill, joins the group for dinner. Even though Jill is quickly accepted by the others, Jean immediately dislikes her. She can't say exactly what it is she doesn't like about Jill, but she thinks,* She makes my skin crawl. *Jean disliked Jill so much that she decided she would leave the group if Jill chose to join it.*

In therapy, Jean was asked to make a list of the qualities that she found annoying about Jill. Her list included the following: *She is too loud, she brags about what she has, she brags about her education, she talks too much, she kept making the others laugh, she had everyone's attention, and she even flirted with the wait staff.*

Jean was unaware of all she was revealing about herself. The qualities she cited about Jill are qualities she herself possesses but remains unaware of. Her therapist pointed out to Jean that she has a tendency to boast about what she possesses and what she has accomplished. The therapist also told her that sometimes her voice is loud and that she has the ability to entertain others and bring attention to herself. Jean denied what the therapist was telling her. The therapist offered up examples of her behavior and also pointed out that these are not necessarily bad traits. When she can recognize and accept them in herself, she will not be bothered when she encounters them in others.

Another example that many face today is the following:

> *Claire and Rob are told that the son of one of their friends has announced that he is gay. Rob is angry. He makes it clear that this young man is no longer welcome in their home. He mocks the young man and calls him hateful names, saying he wants nothing to do with him because he has hurt his family. Six months later Rob admits to a homosexual relationship that he has kept quiet and denied for years.*

Witnessing an unusually strong emotional response is one way to recognize shadow traits in someone. In the first example, Jean takes an immediate dislike to Jill. Her feelings about Jill bother her enough to become the topic of a therapy session. Rob has a hateful reaction to his friends' son being gay because it is like looking in a mirror and seeing something he hates about himself. Rob has clearly not come to terms with his shadow self. He cannot accept his friends' son because he cannot accept what he is ashamed of in himself.

A great deal of information is available about the shadow self. You might enjoy researching the subject yourself. I would like to direct my reader to take a personality test online at my website *www.patriciadanks.com.*

MY PERCEPTIONS *plus*	MY BELIEFS *create*	MY OWN PERSONAL TRUTHS

What are perceptions?
• *What I have learned from:*
  • Family
  • Friends
  • Teachers
  • Senses
  • Religion
	What are beliefs?
	• *My* interpretation of what I have learned
	• The way I believe things *should* be
	• The rules I live by
		What are personal truths?
		• My moral beliefs
		• My code of ethics
		• The judgments I make
		  • Right or wrong
		  • Good or bad

Related words: • Education • Experience • Knowledge • Understanding • Intelligence	*Related words:* • Thoughts • Opinions • Attitudes • Rules • Views 	*Related words:* • Morality • Principles • Values • Wisdom • Code of ethics 
About perceptions: • Core perceptions are in place by the age of eight • My perceptions are always changing because I am always experiencing	*About beliefs:* • My beliefs are always changing because I am constantly interpreting new life lessons and experiences	*About personal truth:* • It is created by the combination of my perceptions and beliefs • My personal truth is always evolving
 *Expressing perceptions, beliefs, and personal truths:* Say "*I think,*" not "*I feel*"		

produce **MY FEELINGS**	*determine* **MY BEHAVIOR**

What are feelings?
• Feelings are felt in the body
  • I *am* happy
  I *feel happy*
  • I *am* disappointed
  I *feel disappointed*
	What is my behavior?
	• What I decide to do
	  • Actions I decide to take
	  • Statements I decide to make
	  • Interaction with others

Related words:
• Negative:
  • Afraid
  • Resentful
  • Angry
  • Depressed
  • Bored
  • Apprehensive
  • Stressed
  • Disappointed
• Positive:
  • Cautious
  • Excited
  • Hopeful
  • Relieved
  • Proud
  • Grateful
  • Flirty
  • Hungry
	Rules of behavior:
	• Rule #1: I choose my behavior
	• Rule #2: Only I can change my behavior
	• Rule #3: I am responsible for my behavior

About feelings:
• My feelings are an emotional reaction to my thoughts about about the events and experiences in my life
• My feelings are always valid
• Feelings cannot be judged right or wrong

	About behavior:
	• My behavior is judged to be:
	  • Right
	    • Acceptable
	    • Honorable
	  • Wrong
	    • Immoral
	    • Criminal

Expressing feelings: Say "*I feel,*" or "*I am*"	***Model sentence:*** I feel __________ because I think __________, so I'm going to __________.

Chapter 5

It's All About You

Allow yourself to think only those thoughts that match your principles and can bear the bright light of day. Day by day, your choices, your thoughts, your actions fashion the person you become. Your integrity determines your destiny.

Heraclitus, Greek philosopher

You have the power to change

Clients have asked me if I think anyone ever really changes. My experience tells me that most people can change their behavior, but it is not always an easy task. It seems to me that change depends on how ingrained a behavior is. However, the person who needs to change must want to change. After that, she needs an average of six months of continual focus on the behavior she wants to change to make noticeable changes. Based on my experience with clients, it takes two years for the new behavior to be established. This does not necessarily mean two years of therapy, but rather two years to focus on the behavior and be mindful of making choices in favor of the change. Awareness does not make the change; concentrated effort does. A person may be aware that her eating habits are compromising her health. She might learn better ways to shop and prepare food. Yet this awareness will not improve her health, unless she develops a strategy for change and acts on it.

Another person might realize that he has problems managing his anger. Being willing to confess to others that he has a temper does not effect change. Understanding the nature of his anger and learning to change his relationship with anger is what will make the difference. Similarly, if you want to learn to play the piano, others will know that you are learning (and they might find it annoying). In six months you will be able to play a recognizable tune from memory. But to read notes and play without noticeable mistakes to entertain others takes about two years of effort and regular practice. Some will quickly gain skill while others will make little progress, depending on their natural ability, dedication to playing well, and willingness to practice. This is also true of changing one's behavior.

But change is certainly possible. I have witnessed much change in my clients over the years as well as in myself. But change doesn't just happen because it is a good idea. Positive change begins with honest self-reflection to identify beliefs, feelings, and personality traits. It is also important that the person trying to change understand the available behavior options.

It is not unusual for an individual to enter into the therapy process with the stated goal of changing his home, social, or work environment. Sometimes, if another person is involved, that other is not supportive and will not come to therapy with the client. The lack of support and participation of the other will not, necessarily, stop the process of change. If you make a commitment to personal change, it will affect everyone around you. This is not a new concept or idea, but to some it still sounds far-fetched. With some guidance, you can effect change by changing yourself, because your life is about you. Now, I don't say this because I believe that your life is about you always getting what you want and being in a continuous state of happiness. But if you are to take personal responsibility, experience personal growth, and exercise self-control, your focus must be on you, not on others. The way you choose to live your life is shaped by your personality, your decisions, and your attitudes about yourself and others in your environment.

To make long-term positive change you must be willing to analyze yourself. Wait! Don't close the book. "Analyze" is not a bad word. It means to separate a whole into its component parts.

To better understand the whole personality, we must understand the relationship between the different parts of the personality. We are looking at the components of behavior, perceptions, beliefs, feelings, and actions and the way these components relate to each other, to determine how we relate to the world we live in. This is a method that, at first, is difficult to understand because it flies in the face of how most of us have learned to think about behavior. In my therapy practice, I find that it takes an individual three sessions to understand what this means and months of practice to competently make use of it. I recommend that you re-read the words immediately above until they are clear to you and you can begin to analyze your behavior. Take care, though, and do not attempt to analyze others. Their behavior is theirs to review; you will be more than busy trying to understand yourself.

Overview

Perception is the ground floor. It gives birth to your thoughts, opinions, and beliefs. Your thoughts stimulate your feelings, and your decisions to act on your feelings will affect your behavior. Others in your life are affected by you and what you do. Likewise, their perceptions, thoughts, truths, feelings, and behavior reflect them and not you. Unless another has the legal right to make your decisions, you are responsible for your behavior and your life decisions. The same is true for others. You are not responsible for the decisions, feelings, or behavior of another person, unless you are their legal guardian.

Because humans function and relate within systems, when you change your behavior, it will affect the system, whether it is a marriage, a family, a workplace, or any group of which you are a part. Your commitment to change your behavior will change the way the system functions. It is true that the system may not change to your satisfaction or benefit, but it will change. The result will indicate to you whether you want to continue as part of the system. You will experience the empowering effect of managing your own behavior and the way it will encourage change in others if they desire to be in a relationship with you. In this sense *it is all about you.*

Perception

Every child is different. The way he experiences life is unique. As one goes through life, it is important to realize that no two people remember or experience life in the same way. Everyone has their own prism through which he views the world. Children, who grow up in the same environment, with the same parents and siblings, do not have the same perception of that experience.

The manner in which you perceive the world is influenced by your personality type as well as your experience of life. Psychologist Alfred Adler's work shows that each sibling in a family is affected in a different way, depending on the order in which he was born. Was he the oldest, the middle child, or the youngest? When someone is an only child in a family, his experience is quite different than a child who grows up with siblings.

Even though they may have many similarities, siblings are

very different. Emotional and psychological make-up is formed by many variables, including each person's place in the family order. For instance, my sister, born sixteen years after me, has a completely different understanding of and relationship with our parents. I remember our parents as a young couple in their twenties, while my sister remembers them in their forties and fifties. My sister has a different memory of childhood, as the younger sister growing up in the 1960s and 1970s. I, the oldest sister, grew up in the 1940s and 1950s. Many studies and books are available to the reader that fully develop the theory of birth order.

Senses play a vital role in perception. Everything you have ever seen, heard, touched, tasted, or felt has influenced your perception of your environment. Every person you have ever met—your parents, extended family, schoolmates, playmates, teachers, friends, and enemies, and even those you cannot remember—has influenced your perception. Everything you have read or learned from others and every place you have visited or traveled has contributed to the way you view life.

Another and more subtle way people perceive is through intuition. This form of perceiving is commonly known as *reading between the lines* and is considered another way of *knowing* without using the senses. When you intuit a belief, you have a strong sense that something is real or true in spite of a lack of noticeable cues. For instance, intuitive people might know that a new acquaintance will become their good friend without any outward cue. One woman tells the story of meeting her best friend. Before she said a word or had eye contact with the other woman, she felt drawn and connected to her. Intuition makes it possible for a person to know if someone is exaggerating or untruthful without any visible proof. When we walk into a room, we can know whether we are welcome by the feel of the experience. On the other hand, even if someone says "Welcome," we might hear what they say but know they mean something different. The way a person feels and acts in the world is rooted in his perceptions of his personal experiences.

Opinions and beliefs

In many cultures the age of reason is about seven or eight years of age. By then we have learned the rules. We know what family and friends expect from us and we have a nascent understanding of right and wrong. In Robert Fulghum's book *All I Really Need to Know I learned in Kindergarten*, he provides an excellent commentary on the value of what we learn by the age of six. By the age of eight the seeds of societal expectations have been planted. We learn how and whether we are valued. We learn those behaviors that bring us praise and those that result in pain or rejection. We have a rudimentary moral code in place and know how things should be.

However, be aware that the perceptions and moral code of an eight-year-old are quite limited compared to that of an adult and, unexamined or unquestioned, these perceptions and moral code cannot mature. Many early rules or beliefs are illogical and do not carry over into adulthood. For instance, a child does not have the freedom to make decisions that are not approved by a parent. Yet, as an adult, he does not need a parent's approval to make decisions. All of us have encountered at one time or other a loud and overbearing person with strong fixed opinions. This type, who is always absolutely sure of his point of view, is typically expressing unexamined fundamental and literal beliefs from his family, culture, religion, or politics. His assumption is that he is always right, and he does not ever consider another point of view. This person speaks with the certainty of a child defending the existence of Santa Claus.

Personal and collective truth

Perception is the basis of one's beliefs, and beliefs are the foundation of personal truth. Personal truth is a collection of beliefs that are deemed factual, correct, or authentic by us. These beliefs shape our perspective or the way we think about things. Because personal truth is based in our personal beliefs and these beliefs come from our perceptions, each person's beliefs differ from those of others. A healthy and mature person will recognize that their personal truth, like their perceptions, is always changing. A friend once said to me . . . *and that's what I think, but ask me again next week because I might change my mind.* This does not reflect a fickle person who flip-flops back and forth, but a woman who is an avid reader and interesting conversationalist. She is always learning and expanding her understanding of her reality.

When interacting with others, people are most comfortable when their personal truth is reflected back to them. When we are with others who share similar truths, we are not challenged and, thus, are comfortable being with those persons. However, when we are not challenged to question our beliefs, our personal truth does not expand and mature. It can be uncomfortable to have our truth challenged by someone who has another view and makes a good case for it. It is embarrassing to belabor a point only to find that we can't support our view with facts. Everyone must examine their personal truth in order to have a mature and intelligent exchange with another.

We quickly learn that our truth may not be shared by others. When we can allow another person to disagree with our fundamental truths, we may find value in his perspective. People learn from listening to and hearing others. I can never assume that I am right while the other is wrong. I am wiser to realize there are many views of truth. One truth does not necessarily cancel the other; instead, each expands the other. It is best to assume a broader position, such as:

- My experience is unique; I do not expect you to share my view.
- It is natural for us to have different views; I'm interested in yours.
- Neither of us has the whole truth; let's see where we agree.
- I'm interested in your story; how did you come to your opinion?
- I do not have expectations of what you should believe.

Just as there is a personal truth, there is a collective or greater truth. Prophets and spiritual leaders have teased out truths that relate to a people or a culture for millennia. An awareness of truth is the basis of spiritual beliefs and cultural taboos. Holy books such as the Torah, Bible, Qur'an, Bhagavad-Gita, and the Upanishads are believed to contain the greater truth expressed through the word of God or holy prophets. Truth, in this sense, is synonymous with the holy—with God. There is a natural yearning for one to know the ultimate truth, to be in union with the divine. When our personal truth is challenged, or when we realize that our personal belief is not in line with truth, we feel threatened. This discomfort goes against a natural desire to be right, to be united with truth.

It is helpful to understand that no one person can perceive the whole of truth. Many people report spiritual experiences in which they gain extraordinary insights into truth. Usually it is difficult for them to describe the event as they experienced it, because they cannot relate it to other life experiences or they do not have language that adequately represents the experience. I believe that we need a lifetime of conversations and exchanges of personal truth to enrich our understanding of divine truth.

We expand our personal truth by participating in activities such as reading, watching documentary films, learning world history and geography, doing research, and traveling. We gather information in any way available to us. It is always wise to learn about the other, whether it is the other political party, the other religion, or another culture or language. Learning about the other will either challenge or confirm our beliefs. Humans are curious, and our nature is to investigate and discover. Wise people who have eighty or ninety years of life experience will tell you they continue to learn and realize that, after a lifetime, they know very little of all there is to know.

Feelings

You may sigh at the mention of feelings. In fact, you may feel impatient or bored with the thought of addressing the subject at all. The word "feeling" is used and misused in many ways, and you may be tired of the word. But, it is important to grasp an awareness of this very important phenomenon. I will use a specific definition for this discussion: *A feeling is a kind of awareness, or a level of consciousness, that is felt in the body.* In this respect, I am not referring to the physical sensation that is felt when there is a stimulation of the skin or a muscle. Rather, I am directing you to think of feeling as a sensation resulting from an emotional stimulus that is felt somewhere in the body. Amber's experience emphasizes this point:

> *Amber is looking forward to her first day at a new job. She is excited and eager to enter into a new environment, meet new people, and work in her chosen field. As she approaches the door*

> *of her new building, she suddenly experiences a wave of nausea and feels light-headed. She recognizes that this discomfort is her body informing her of a deeper emotional response to her first day in a new environment. Suddenly she feels fearful, unsure of herself, and doubtful. The emotional sensation moves to her neck and upper back, and she begins to feel tingling in her arms and chest muscles and the hint of a developing migraine.*

Although Amber enjoys the feelings of excitement and eagerness that come with anticipating her new job, she does not like the physical feelings that seem to appear from nowhere. Amber has learned to listen to her body. She recognizes these feelings as her body's response to an unacknowledged or unidentified feeling. Amber identifies her feelings as doubt and fear. She takes a deep breath and looks for a place to sit for a moment until she calms down. She acknowledges her feelings by admitting that she is afraid. In silent self-talk, she reminds herself that she will do well. She is qualified for this job, she tells herself, and can do the work. She imagines that she will feel welcome and comfortable. Once she feels calm, she continues to her new workplace.

Deep emotional feelings can appear unannounced. They seem to flood up from someplace deep within and overwhelm us. It is my belief that these feelings come from an unconscious place and that they are stimulated by unidentified thoughts or beliefs related to an experience or perception that occurs in the present. These feelings reflect an honest appraisal of what is going on in our psyche, or soul. They can be identified through an honest reflection on what is happening inside of us at the time. Often, the thoughts behind these feelings are immature beliefs that we have not processed as an adult.

For instance, Amber might be harboring beliefs that she will fail and not be able to perform to her employer's standards. In identifying these thoughts, she can dispel them by recalling other times when she has experienced these feelings without terrible consequences. She contrasts these childish thoughts with what she has accepted as truth: she is confident and capable, even though there is a possibility that she will feel awkward during this first day. She will remind herself that others are generally unaware of her awkwardness and will welcome her into this new environment. By concentrating on her positive past experiences, she is able to compose herself.

Emotional feelings manifest as physical feelings. Sometimes you might feel an ache or pain somewhere in your body before you are conscious of an emotional feeling. For instance, a headache might be your first warning that you are worrying too much. A stomachache or nausea might alert you to a feeling of fear or foreboding. You will recognize that you are anxious when your pulse quickens and you can hear your heart beat and feel your chest tighten. You might begin to sweat or feel lightheaded. Maybe you will hold your breath. If you are overwhelmed with responsibility, you might develop pain in your back, shoulders, or neck area. You might feel fear, shame, guilt, and loneliness in your abdomen. If a feeling like fear or shame lasts for days, months, or years, the physical pain is considered chronic.

Most of us are familiar with the expression: *Listen to your body and let it tell you what you need.* We have also learned that many of us are disconnected or out of touch with our bodies. Exciting new research is helping us understand the variety of ways we perceive information. We are learning that neurotransmitter cells in the gut make possible another way of knowing as well as those neurotransmitters found in the brain. The emotions and feelings that we experience give us an indication of how things truly are with us.

You might experience many feelings at once affecting many places in your body. Sometimes when we experience trauma or grief the feelings are so intense that our brains mercifully block them. Although we know that we are feeling something, we cannot experience its full intensity. Instead, we are numb to all that is happening around us. Sometimes weeks after a funeral or a traumatic event, a person may not remember details of the event. It is as if our body protects us from the intensity of our feelings as a way of protecting the integrity of our psyche.

Feelings alert one to personal truth and possible threats to one's integrity. Feelings are a natural way to determine emotional and spiritual well-being. They are a way for us to know who we are. For this reason one can say *I am* when expressing an emotional feeling: *I am afraid* or *I am so sorry.* We often use physical terms to describe emotional states: *I'm just sick about what I did* or *It just breaks my heart to hear that.* At some deeper level, we do know the connection between our emotional state and our physical state.

Feelings and thoughts and beliefs are not interchangeable. They are different components of the personality that describe different processes. Thoughts express beliefs, opinions, and judgments, while feelings express a person's emotional state of being. For instance, Amber could say *I am nervous* to express her feeling. But she cannot express it as a thought, for example: *I think nervous.* Neither can she rightfully say *I feel this is the right workplace for me,* because her statement is an opinion and not a feeling—she cannot say, *I am this is the right workplace for me.* But she can say, *I think this is the right workplace for me, even though I am nervous.*

It is important to remember that feelings come from beliefs. Opinions, judgments, beliefs, and thoughts are cognitive processes that involve intellectual activity. These produce feelings—emotional responses that are felt in the body. Feelings are stimulated by one's thoughts, which might be irrational or illogical. Possibly Amber's feelings are telling her something altogether different than her thoughts. Her feelings may be telling her that this is not the right workplace, even though she thinks it is. After working there for thirty days, she may realize her feelings were actually a premonition.

Even though learning to identify feelings is a necessary part of choosing healthy behavior, sometimes the feeling that needs to be identified is buried so deep that we cannot access it. Instead, it manifests as raw emotion and, because it is unrecognized, we act unconsciously and impulsively. A good example of this is seen in the interaction between Scott and his father, Mike:

> *Mike grew up in the 1980s in a religious family where the well-defined rules were enforced. Mike's father was an untreated alcoholic who worked hard during the week and drank on the weekends. He was also the disciplinarian of the family. He loved his children but, with his work hours and his alcoholism, he rarely had time or energy to demonstrate his good feelings for his children. He ruled with an iron fist and did not ask questions. If Mike got out of line, the result was a rash of rage and even physical violence from his father.*
>
> *Mike vowed to be a better father when he had children, promising himself he would never abuse them. He was not going to be like his father. Twenty-five years later, Mike is the father of a fifteen-year-old son, Scott. True to his word, Mike is a good parent. Scott is a happy teen and a good student who is popular with his many friends. Mike has encouraged him to make his own decisions and has been his advocate. Recently, though, a rift seems to be growing between them. Mike is becoming short-tempered and irritable around his son. He finds fault with his behavior and even teases him in a mocking way. One day Scott comes home to announce that he has been chosen to receive a sports award. Mike barely acknowledges Scott's ex-*

citement. Later, when passing Scott's bedroom, Mike flies into a rage because the room is messy. What's the matter? What are you so pissed about? *Scott asks his father. Mike hits his son, cutting his mouth, and Scott is dumbfounded. Mike goes to his room and slams the door.*

What just happened? Believe it or not, this is a common family dynamic. If this family came to me for counseling, my first question would be: *What was life like for you at age fifteen, Mike?* All those years that Mike has spent making a conscious effort to be a good parent have paid off for him. His happy and successful son is a sign that he has succeeded. Mike is a good father. But as he observes the wonderful life he has created for his rapidly maturing son, a little voice inside of Mike is quietly saying, *Hey, wait a minute, this isn't fair—I deserved this life. Why didn't I have reassurance from my father? Why didn't I get help with my schoolwork?* And, finally: *Why didn't I get an award?*

In essence, his emotion is giving voice to his childhood experiences and years of hurt. Mike is unconsciously jealous of his son. His rage is rooted in information that is not consciously available to him, and it has nothing to do with Scott or his messy room. When this is brought to his consciousness in the session, Mike is appalled at what he, at first, thinks is a ridiculous suggestion. Yet as he talks about it, his eyes fill with tears as he remembers his teen years. He can admit that, even though his jealousy and resentment are irrational, making no sense to him, the theory has some validity. Mike needs to acknowledge these feelings in order to be at ease with his son's accomplishments. In some ways he needs to grieve the childhood he never had to become free enough to share in the childhood he has created for his own son. His raw emotion signaled to him that he has not grieved or worked through past hurts and resentments.

This story is an example of unconscious experience being brought to light, where it can be examined and identified as irrational. With self-awareness, Mike can choose behavior that makes more sense and avoid reacting with rage.

Guilt

Guilt is both a feeling and a judgment. It may be the most pervasive feeling I am confronted with in therapy. Guilty thoughts seem to pull us down into depression more than anything else. First, let us be clear: *Others do not make you feel guilty.* You feel guilty because of what you think about your behavior. I like to differentiate between healthy guilt and neurotic guilt. Healthy guilt arises when you have behaved in a way that betrays your sense of morality and your personal values. This feeling is important because it keeps you on track in becoming and acting like the person you are meant to be. Healthy guilt reminds you that you are human and, as such, are prone to mistakes and oversights. Like everyone else, you are capable of doing terrible things. We all have patterns of behavior that we need to change. When we say or do something to another, or to ourselves, that we know is wrong, we feel guilty. Our feelings of guilt tell us that we have betrayed our values and our own basic moral code.

On the other hand, neurotic guilt arises when we act in a way that betrays another's values or expectations. The other feels hurt because he thinks you should do what he wants or expects. You, instead, choose to do something different, according to your beliefs. The other gets angry and blames you for doing the wrong thing. Now, you may feel guilty because you have made the other unhappy. But this is not rational thinking, since you cannot make the other unhappy. Whether or not he is happy is up to him, not you. If he continues thinking that others should act according to his rules, rather than their own rules, he will always be unhappy when others do not do as he wants them to. But you want to follow your conscience, not his. His unhappiness is not a reason for you to change your mind and do as he expects. Your decision must be rooted in your own sense of right and wrong, not someone else's. We have learned much about this dynamic from addiction treatment centers. Let's look at Sara's situation:

> *A talented, intelligent young woman of twenty-two, Sara has a job that she finds satisfactory, but it is not one that she wants for a career. She tends to stay out late with friends, often coming home well after midnight. Usually, she has several alcoholic drinks with her friends. Sara knows she is compromising her work and asks her mother to call her in the morning to make sure she is awake. Sara's mother refuses to call her, saying she does not want to be responsible for Sara getting up. Sara eventually loses her job, and she blames her mother.*

Sara's mother certainly made the right decision. And she has no reason to feel guilty. In fact, if Sara's mother had refused to coax her awake at the age of twelve, Sara might have taken on the responsibility of getting herself up at that time. If her mother feels guilty, it is because she is suffering the consequences of Sara's behavior, and her feeling of guilt is unhealthy. Let's change the scenario a little to show healthy guilt:

> *Sara is a conscientious worker. She tries to get to work fifteen minutes early every day because she does not like to be late. One morning her car will not start. Sara knows that her mother is home and calls to ask her for assistance. Sara's mother says she can't give her a ride. She explains that it is her day off and she*

wants to relax, instead of spending an hour going to and from Sara's workplace. After the call, Sara's mother feels guilty and has an inner conflict. More than anything, she wants to stay at home, but she is committed to being there for her daughter. She realizes that her guilty feelings are making her too uncomfortable, and she will not enjoy being at home when her daughter needs her. Sara's mother has a choice: she can let her daughter solve her problem on her own or she can give up her immediate comfort to help Sara.

In both instances, Sara's mother must make a decision. In the first example, she says No, because the request is not in keeping with her value that her daughter be responsible for herself. To feel guilty because Sara might be disappointed is unhealthy. But, in the second example, Sara's mother might say Yes. In this case, her healthy guilt prompts her to do the right thing according to her values. It is important to note that Sara does not make her mother feel guilty. Rather, her mother's guilt comes from the misalignment between her feelings, her values, and her actions. We feel healthy guilt when our actions betray our personal values. To determine whether our actions deserve healthy guilt, you can reflect on your behavior and ask yourself: *Is what I did wrong? Did I know it was wrong when I did it? Knowing it was wrong, did I choose to do it anyway?*

Memory often produces unhealthy guilt. As one grows older and wiser, it is common to recall many poor decisions and thoughtless actions from the past. But it is important to remember that we change and grow over the years. Our perceptions of the past are very different than they were twenty or thirty years ago. Using the exercise above, you can put things in perspective. It is important to judge past actions in the context of your understanding of the situation and the resources you had at that time. When you realize that you did something wrong because you were uncaring, greedy, or selfish, then it is necessary to make amends. However, if you did the best you could at the time, using the resources available to you, it is necessary to forgive yourself and be thankful for what you have learned since then. If you need to make amends, and it is not possible because the other is dead or your amends will cause embarrassment or harm to them, you can choose to do something to help someone else in a similar situation. Consider the following:

> *Brittany did not get along with her mother. They argued continually and did not enjoy being together. When Brittany went to school, she chose not to come home for holidays and, in her second year of college, she got an apartment and permanently moved out of her mother's house. She rarely called and did not share her life experiences with her mother.*
>
> *The year after Brittany moved out, her mother was stricken with terminal cancer and died following a short and painful illness. Although she called Brittany several times, Brittany chose not to return her calls. Brittany did not know about her mother's illness.*

After her mother's death, Brittany was confused by the terrible sadness that overtook her and her feelings of loneliness. She became depressed, crying every day, suffering from insomnia, losing her appetite, and no longer enjoying her activities or friends. When Brittany sought grief counseling, she realized that she was the cause of much of the tension between her and her mother. She learned that her mother had stress in her work and her relationships. She had been unaware that her mother needed her love and affection as much as she needed her mother's. She had not had the maturity to realize that her mother had a life and relationships apart from her own.

Brittany felt intensely guilty and did not know how to reconcile with her mother. She wrote a letter of apology to her mother, but this did not make much of a difference, and she did not feel any better. Eventually she was recommended as a companion to a homebound elderly woman and formed a strong friendship with her. She shopped for groceries for the woman weekly and ran other essential errands. She told the woman about her activities and shared her experiences with her. Every holiday, she spent an hour or more with her. Although Brittany could never undo the pain she had caused her mother, she reconciled the guilt within herself by doing for someone else what she wished she had done for her mother.

When the wrong is reconciled, the guilty feeling will lessen and you will find relief.

Behavior

Your behavior is rooted in your feelings. You act out your feelings in two ways: either you react to your feelings or you recognize them and choose how you want to respond. Behavior is a choice, even though actions are prompted by and rooted in emotion. An analogy: fuel provides energy for your car engine to run, but the car does not move until you make some decisions about the accelerator, emergency brake, and gears. The driver must provide the intention. Similarly, feelings provide an impulse to react or respond, but you must provide intention. You are the one who must decide what to do with the energy provided by the impulse. To be *response-able,* a person must make a decision about expressing his feelings. Other people are not responsible for your behavior any more than the car next to you on the freeway makes your car go faster. Thus, comments such as, *He made me do it* or *You made me hit you with your stupid demands* are just not true. This makes as much sense as if you were to say, *My car was speeding because the car next to me was going too slow.* Rather, your car was speeding because you made a decision to press down on the accelerator.

Unlike feelings, actions can be judged good or bad, right or wrong. What you do can affect your surroundings and the people in your life in profound ways. It is important to understand that behavior has consequences. When we choose a behavior, we are responsible for the natural consequences that follow. Cultures and societies develop rules, expectations, and laws to help us live well together. There are consequences when we break a law—when our behavior is not in keeping with the expectations of our society.

Blame

When someone says Don't blame me, chances are she means: *Don't ask me to take responsibility. I don't want anyone to know I'm responsible, and you should overlook what I've done.* Or blame is employed when a person is projecting her responsibility onto another. When you are honest about your behavior and take responsibility for yourself, there is no reason to blame another. A good example of this is when one person nags another. None of us like to be nagged, and it is irritating when someone continually tells us what to do. It is easy to blame someone for nagging us. Yet we create our own nag. If I know what I am responsible for, I will do it, without being asked. If I do not know what I'm responsible for, it is fair that someone tell me. But, if I agree to do something, and I do it, nobody will need to ask me again. However, if I do not do it, I will be asked again and again. I have created a nag, and I want to blame that person for nagging me. If, on the other hand, there are consequences to my irresponsibility, I might do what is right without any reminder. The nag, on the other hand, must decide whether she wants to be a nag and continue to ask me and remind me. Or she might ask one time if I will do something. If I do not do it, I should take the consequences. A common example is seen in the homes of many teens:

> *Mother asks son and daughter to pick up their shoes and schoolbags and take them out of the family room and put them away. The teens do not acknowledge her request. She asks again. They do not respond. She asks again. No response.*

A better way:

> *Mother asks son and daughter to pick up their shoes and schoolbags and take them out of the family room and put them away. The teens do not acknowledge her request. Mom picks up their things and puts them in a box in the garage. The box collects everything the teens do not put away. Eventually the teens tire of going to the garage to get their things and make an effort to keep them out of their mother's hands.*

Anger and rage

So many excellent books are available that address anger that it is not necessary to discuss the topic in full here. But it is important to define it in a way that helps us to fit anger management into the discussion. If you want to understand your anger and manage it, it is necessary to know that anger is a secondary feeling. Underlying anger are other hurtful primary feelings such as disappointment, frustration, resentment, fear, guilt, jealousy, embarrassment, and poor self-esteem. To address anger, a person must first identify these primary feelings and question whether or not they are based in rational thought. For instance, if a person is made the brunt of a joke, he might strike out in anger. Underlying his anger might be a belief he is harboring that he is foolish or not as worthy as those teasing him and a fear that others have discovered his real self. Even though the belief is untrue, the fear is very real and produces anger that he acts out impulsively.

Another example: *disappointment is related to expectations.* If you learn that you get angry when you are disappointed, you will also learn that when you adjust your expectations, you can stop being disappointed. For example:

> *Karl is angry. He had left work early to meet his wife at their son's school for a conference. His wife was not at the school when he arrived. He waited with his son for twenty minutes and then left in a huff, slamming the car door and speeding out of the parking lot. He spoke sarcastically to his son, telling him to be quiet and leave him alone.*

Karl does not know how to manage his anger, and this is why he left the school, blaming his wife for making them miss the conference. He might say she is selfish and inconsiderate. He might accuse her of doing or thinking something that is not true. However, if Karl learns to manage his behavior, he will realize that his expectations—that his wife should arrive at the school at the same time he did—are too rigid. His expectation is reasonable, but there are many reasons that she did not show up when he expected her. Underlying Karl's anger is his disappointment that his wife did not meet his expectations. When he realizes that he cannot control the outcome of another's behavior, he will be able to accept the disappointment and frustration he feels. He can then decide how he wants to respond to these feelings. His son and wife are not the cause of his anger.

To blame another person for making you angry is only a quick fix, and it will not make you feel better. To adjust your irrational thought process is more difficult, but much more long-lasting. It is not unusual for a person to become angry because he is too embarrassed to admit that he is feeling disappointed or resentful.

Angry behavior can be reactive and impulsive or premeditated. It is common for a person to harbor hateful thoughts about a person or an event, escalating his anger over a period of time. Replaying the event in his mind causes stress and depression. Harboring hurtful or hateful feelings can end in a premeditated act of revenge which, uninterrupted, can lead to criminal behavior. Note, though, that the behavior begins not with another person, but in his own mind. Generally, a third person, neutral to the event, is needed to help the angry person think through the process. When we are severely stressed, thinking is impaired and a third person can help resolve the issue, because she is not a part of the problem and does not share the difficult feelings.

It is important to know the difference between anger and rage. Everyone feels angry at times; it is not wrong to feel angry, but there are appropriate ways to express it. Rage, however, is different. Rage is an impulsive action associated with life-and-death situations. Disconnected from rational thought, rage is rarely an appropriate response in our everyday lives. It is a primitive response necessary to keep a human or animal alive. In primitive societies, rage gave humans the energy to kill a beast for food or protect the clan. But rage can be dangerous in a community or a home. Most murders are a result of someone's rage. It is clear that rage is never appropriate in family quarrels.

A primitive and infantile reaction, rage is only appropriate in a family setting when an infant is responding to hunger or pain. Physical expression of rage is distinct from anger in that it is spontaneous. An infant can quickly change from cooing sweetness to an all-consuming rage. A baby's facial expression will change to a flushed red color, she will make fists with her hands, her whole body will engage in screaming until she is comforted and her needs are met. She doesn't think about it because she does not yet possess that cognitive ability. It is imperative that she do this to relay the message of life and death to those around her. A baby cannot think rationally and have the expectation that her needs will be met. She will rage until her internal pain dissipates. A baby is helpless and cannot obtain food or water for herself. If her cries do not lead to rescue, she will die. Take the above scenario and apply it to this thirty-year-old woman:

> *Shelby got a call from her girlfriend, who said that she had seen Shelby's husband at a coffee shop that morning. He was sitting at a table with a woman the friend did not recognize. She described the woman, her clothing, and her mannerisms. The friend questioned who this woman might be.*
>
> *Shelby felt punched in the gut and became angry. She hung up the phone and began to scream. She threw her cell phone against a wall, shouted profanities, and called her husband nasty names. She jumped in her car to go and find him. When she got to the coffee shop, her husband was standing alone in the parking lot. She got out of the car, began to pummel his chest, and screamed, You cheating . . .*

This type of scene happens all the time. What is wrong with it? Well, Shelby's behavior is irrational. This is not a life-and-death problem, but Shelby acts as if it is. Her whole body is engaged. She screams and throws things in an infantile way. She does not stop to reflect on the situation; she does not think it through. Her husband's infidelity is the only possibility Shelby considers. She does not allow time to reflect on her feelings and fears before confronting him and, when she does, it is not a conversation. If, in fact, he is being unfaithful, her impulsive reaction does nothing to help them resolve their issues. If he is not being unfaithful, she appears to be a crazy out-of-control woman.

It is possible Shelby had a previous relationship with an unfaithful partner and may now believe that her husband, given a chance, will cheat on her. Maybe he has cheated before, and she thinks he is once again betraying her. Or her behavior may be out of character, because she has become unemployed or ill. If so, it is a warning that she needs to address her other issues. If her husband is merely having lunch with a co-worker, the scene she has created is embarrassing and inappropriate.

If, in fact, her husband is beginning an affair, Shelby's behavior is not helpful and will not improve the situation. Whatever the case, Shelby's rage is inappropriate. She must identify her feelings of fear and insecurity. Doing so will allow her to wait until evening to ask about his luncheon companion. If it becomes clear that the meeting was inappropriate, it becomes even more important for her to manage her angry behavior and make rational choices for herself. Throwing his belongings out the front door might make Shelby feel better in the moment, but her irrational behavior will only work against her. In the long-term, it is better that she act rationally and choose behaviors that will not do harm to either her or her husband. If she is too angry to think clearly, it is best that she seek the support of a third person to talk to.

Rage is only appropriate when someone is in need of extraordinary strength to cope with a real life-and-death event. For example:

> *Tammy is sharing a play date with her friends and their toddlers. The children are frolicking in the shallow end of the*

> *swimming pool with an adult. Tammy is standing on the patio talking with her friends and scanning the pool, when she sees little Monica toddling toward the edge of the deep end. Tammy screams and trips over a deck chair, knocking over food and beverages. She jumps into the pool just as little Monica goes over the edge, pulling her from the water and making sure she is OK. Tammy is shaking all over and trying to tell her friends what she saw, but she is stammering and not making sense. Her heart is beating fast, and she feels faint and needs to sit down.*

You will recognize the primitive physical symptoms of rage. Tammy screams and acts without thinking, and her whole body engages as she jumps into the pool. The difference between this and Shelby's situation is that it is a real life-and-death situation. Reflection and rational thinking will take time and, in this situation, may waste valuable time.

Domestic violence and child abuse are often the result of someone's rage. Since rage signals a life-and-death reaction, people often die or are maimed as a result of it. Rage is not to be confused with anger. Anger is a healthy feeling, and it is normal. Rage in everyday life is not. One does not rage at a teen who comes home late. A mature parent does not rage at a toddler who spills a gallon of milk on the floor. She does not hit, push, or throw the child, and she does not yell, scream, and threaten the child. Rather, she realizes that this is what toddlers do and takes the opportunity to teach the toddler how to pour milk or ask for assistance. Then she has the child help in cleaning up the mess. Yes, she feels frustrated and possibly angry. But she reflects on the situation and chooses an appropriate action.

Behavior is a choice. It is often said that *To decide to do nothing is doing something.* Behavior is prompted by and based in

The Ego

The word "ego" derives from Latin and means "I." Ego defines the conscious part of the psyche. The ego is the conscious part of a person that is motivated by fear of unconsciousness or injury and death. This fear motivates the healthy ego to defend itself from emotional hurt and anxiety through a range of defenses, such as denial of potential hurts or threats or rationalizing—convincing one's self that harmful actions are justified. Sometimes people isolate themselves from people or events that remind them of painful experiences and emotions. Sometimes painful feelings and emotions are transformed into physical pain, as in psychosomatic conditions. We use a range of defenses to protect the ego and form a sense of security that give the illusion of safety and security. This is a natural way for the ego to protect itself from being overwhelmed and destroyed by more negative emotions than it can handle.

It is common when people experience a traumatic event, such as a violent death of a loved one or an assault, or they are a witness to a violent crime, for them to remain calm and quiet, reacting as if what has just happened is not very important. They might even dull the memory of the event so it does not interrupt their conscious reality. But later, when they are stronger, the emotion may seep through their defenses, forcing them to experience the pain as if the event has just happened.

the emotional state. Feelings prompt one to react on impulse or respond with intention. To be *response-able,* a person must make a decision about expressing every feeling. Other people are not responsible for your behavior. Thus, comments such as, *He made me do it* or *You made me angry* are just not true. Behavior is directly related to feelings and is influenced by perception and personal truth. Personal choice determines behavior.

Points to remember about personal responsibility:

- Perception comes from one's experience of the environment and is both sensate and intuitive.
- Personal perception is the sum of everything you have observed, learned, and experienced.
- Personal truth is formed from an assessment of perception.
- Beliefs, opinions, and judgments express personal truth.
- Greater truth is collective and is the truth of a people or a culture.
- Feelings are connected to thoughts, opinions, and expectations, and they are not the result of what others do but of what you think about what others do.
- Feelings are indicators of both emotional distress and well-being.
- Feelings are felt in the body.
- Behavior is rooted in your feelings.
- Guilt is either healthy or neurotic.
- Anger is not a wrong or bad feeling, but the way anger is expressed can be wrong or immoral.
- Rage is rarely an appropriate response to anger.

Chapter 6

Developing a Personal Identity

All the world's a stage,
And all the men and women merely players,
They have their exits and their entrances,
And one man in his time plays many parts.

William Shakespeare, from *As You Like It*

Creating your identity

When you understand the origins of your behavior, it will become evident that much of your identity is your choice. Each of us can become the kind of person we want to be. We are not who others say we are, nor are we limited to fulfilling their expectations of us. Our behavior illuminates our identity. Others judge us through their interpretation of our behavior. Have you ever felt out of place with other people? Are you disappointed in the way you act around others? Do you often feel hurt about what others say to you—or about you? When you have a realistic and positive sense of who you are, you will be less affected by thoughtless criticism and hurtful comments from others. Just as a strong body builds immunity to invading germs, the ego also builds immunity to *invasive and destructive thinking.*

Personality and identity begin to develop at conception. Women who have given birth more than once will agree that each pregnancy, birth, and resulting infant has identifying characteristics that set it apart from the others. Mothers can predict a restless, active baby before it is born and may compare it to an older sibling who is quiet and subdued.

As parents observe their infant, they identify movements, expressions, and physical features that are familial: *Susie has Uncle Art's serious gaze* or *Brandan has ears like his father's.* As we identify genetic traits, it becomes clear that many characteristics of the child are not shared by anyone we know. We begin to see a new identity, someone we have never known before. Each of us is born with genetic similarities to our family. And each of us is born into a story of an era, a culture, and a family into which we have had no input or choice. This phenomenon is unique to each of us and presents a blueprint or an outline for our path in life. Because it involves many decisions that may or may not be in our best interest, I will refer to it as a *birth dilemma*. One might think: *Well, this is a fine kettle of fish!* We are born into a story that is so complicated it will take a lifetime to make sense of it all. But most of this dilemma cannot be changed and is the raw material with which we are expected to build a life. This is both overwhelming and exciting. Each of us must carve a life that is satisfying and, with luck, that allows us to contribute something to society.

Life is not predetermined; we make an infinite number of choices in determining who we will be and how we will live our lives. In personal reflection, we can see the stages of our lives and understand when we began consciously to choose who we will be.

In middle school years, children become aware that they are different than their peers. For most this is uncomfortable, and as part of their separation from their parents, they begin to identify with their peers. To ensure that they are acceptable, they strive for sameness with them. It is important that they wear the right clothes, use the same language, and develop the same gestures and movements that will hold them high in the esteem of their mates. This dynamic continues until early adulthood, when they have more confidence, seek individuality, and appreciate being different from their peers. Because this is a process, each of us does it in our own way and time.

Sometimes, though, a person does not experience this phase of development. Maybe she was raised in a strict family or belief system that discouraged self-expression and individuality and taught her not to trust her environment. Or maybe he had a mother who, suffering hurts from her own past, inflicts on him comments like *You're so dumb* or *You'll never amount to anything* that have left him with a negative and defeated attitude. All of us must develop the self-confidence that allows us to separate from the expectations of our parents. Otherwise, we will continue to judge ourselves according to their expectations.

It is a mistake to create an identity that is based in the expectations of others. Or, as commonly happens, a person may be in a relationship with a controlling person who dictates her behavior. Perhaps life as she knew it collapsed because of the death of a significant other or a divorce. For others a traumatic event like death or divorce may initiate a mid-life transition. For any number of reasons, a person can find herself feeling lost and confused, not knowing what she wants or who she is. At this point, it is a challenge for her to know where to begin to find her identity. To understand this point, let us look at Julie's situation:

> *Like most people, Julie knows she can stand up for herself and is a valuable and good person. But that awareness swirls around inside of her with many other messages that emphasize the opposite. Julie has compared herself to others all of her life, and in her mind she is not quite good enough. She thinks she is not very smart, pretty, or talented. She compares herself to those whom she holds in high esteem and considers the very best, which results in her belief that she is lacking, is inferior in almost ev-*

erything. The memories of negative parental messages, sharp reprimands from teachers, or insults from childhood drown out the compliments and encouragements she has also received. Because the negative comments make a greater emotional impact, she holds onto them and they shape her sense of herself. She pays little attention to praise and compliments, smiling as she discounts them, because she knows they can't be true and, besides, they do not support her belief that she is inferior. Unconsciously, Julie has constructed a belief system that is supported by a lie: I am inferior, and there are limits to what I can do and who I can be. I have a good sense of humor but I am not very intelligent, especially attractive, or interesting. Julie has developed a passable persona that helps her to feel comfortable with friends and coworkers, and she uses her wit to cover up her sense of insecurity.

Committed to a moral life and doing what she believes is right, Julie marries while still in her teens. She is a good wife and mother and is devoted to her family and home. But, inside, she feels empty and lost, almost as if she is living the wrong life. Not grounded in herself, she cannot find her center. She gauges her life according to what others want, or think, or ask of her. When things do not go well, she takes full responsibility for the failure and blames herself. Julie struggles with bouts of depression that begin to affect her ability to function well. She suffers from insomnia, lying awake at night thinking about how her life is all wrong. She cries when she is alone so that others will not see her sadness. She has lost interest in everything that has previously brought her happiness, and she is having difficulty concentrating. Julie decides to enter psychotherapy. In the first months of therapy, Julie admits that she married too young, making a lifetime commitment to the wrong person. She loves being a homemaker but also wants to complete her education.

Julie's story is not unusual. In fact, among the most common themes for people entering therapy is the belief that they are living the wrong life. When people are not living the life they are meant to live, it initiates an affective response such as depression or anxiety or a combination of both. In treating depression or anxiety, my most valuable query has always been the following: *What are you doing that you desperately do not want to do?* or *What are you not doing that you know you need to do?*

These situations do not have simple solutions. To reconcile a life and re-focus takes time and discernment. Dialogue with loved ones is imperative. Everyone in the family system is affected and every person's beliefs and truths are challenged. The family system changes, because friends and family are expected to make monumental adjustments that they have not anticipated. For those who can make the transition with integrity, life improves. But, realistically, some friends and family members do not make these transitions well. Rather, they distance themselves, are unsupportive, and find fault with the person making the changes.

The challenge to change can be met with acceptance of the person trying to change and agreement, or disagreement, with the actual change. For instance if a woman in a religious community decides this life is wrong for her and embraces the life of a lay woman, some friends and family members may respond by saying, *I respect you, but I do not agree with your decision.*

This response is common when a family member gets married or divorced, comes out to the family as gay, or discloses that he is living as a man in a woman's body. These life changes affect family and friends deeply and the decisions are not automatically accepted by loved ones. The person making the change often meets with resistance or anger or even attacks from loved ones. This negative response is not directed at the person because of his decision to reconcile his life. But rather it is because a spouse, family member, or friend cannot support him in living his life in a way that they believe is not right or moral. The spouse or family member must have the ability to reconcile their judgment of the other's actions with their own personal truths and beliefs in order to continue a satisfactory relationship. For instance, they might think: *I don't believe in what you are doing, but I realize it is not my decision. I still have regard for you.*

Most people today understand that prolonged stress and depression take a physical toll on us. Learning to be comfortable with oneself is a must for overall physical and emotional health. Done well, transitions help one grow in wisdom, understanding, and in the ability to offer unconditional love. Generally, a person can try as hard as possible to do a good job of making a major life

The Persona

Persona comes from the Latin word *persona*, which means mask. A persona is a temporary personality developed to dress up the ego to play an important and specific role. A persona is a healthy defense that allows a person to do something he wants to do, when he does not have the confidence or experience to carry it out. For instance, a woman may wear the personas of teacher, mother, girlfriend, and lover—she might also be a volleyball coach or scout leader. A man may wear the persona of engineer, hockey player, husband, and father. Another may wear the persona of bachelor, priest, and friend. In these roles the men and the women may be proficient and successful. Yet if you asked each one, they will tell you they are all of these roles and much more. An emotionally healthy person will integrate his various personas and not identify with only one.

change or transition and still leave a trail of broken hearts and lives. Major life changes often dramatically alter friendships and family alliances. They can become stronger and more intimate, or they can be ruined. You must be true to yourself and live a life that reflects what is best for you. When you live the life that someone else is dictating, you will feel empty and question your self-worth.

Putting on a persona

It is possible for a person who thinks of himself as happy and content to find himself over the course of his life in changing circumstances that he must adapt to. Think of a time when you found yourself in a new environment with new people and different expectations. Such a predicament typically comes at transitional times in our lives. With maturity, we learn to adapt to a new environment within a few days or weeks. Depending on the circumstances, it may take even longer. Newlyweds generally need a year to adjust to living together and managing their life as a couple, even if they have lived together for months or years before marriage. A new employee may take ninety days to get acclimated.

When I first became a therapist, I transitioned from being a youth minister working with teens to a professional concentrating on adults and families. My wardrobe changed from sneakers, jeans, and sweatshirts to casual business dress. I got a new hairstyle, make-up, and eyeglasses. I needed a professional persona to fit my new role.

In dream imagery, clothing and accessories represent a persona. Unlike a false self, a persona is a way to dress up our egos to make ourselves presentable and comfortable in a specific role. Sometimes we evolve through several different personas in one day. For instance, in one day I am wife, mother, grandmother, great-grandmother, writer, therapist, and co-worker. If I join girlfriends for lunch, I take on still another persona. I move comfortably from one role to another, often changing my clothing, conversation style, and sense of humor as I transition. I don't talk with clients in the same way I talk with my girlfriends. I never speak intimately with casual friends in the way that I do with my husband. I try not to talk with my grown children as if they are clients (although at times I do), and I don't talk with my husband as if he were a co-worker.

The healthy ego can smoothly move from one persona to the next because one does not deny the existence of the other and each utilizes different facets of the ego to create harmony with the environment. When a person moves into a new circumstance, he observes others to understand the norms and adjusts his personality to blend in. When a person cannot do this comfortably, he might say, *I feel out of place there. This just isn't me.* Either he must create a persona that will work for him, be uncomfortable in that situation, or avoid the situation altogether. This can have a profound effect on a life. For instance, if a young freshman feels uncomfortable at her university campus, she may quit school rather than find a way to adapt to homesickness and her new routine and friends.

If I had not developed a therapist persona, I would not have felt comfortable in my new role and done as well. A persona helps us to define personal boundaries and choose appropriate behavior. Be aware, though, that a new persona is uncomfortable. It can feel phony and look that way to others. Like a new hairstyle that draws attention and comments from friends, your new persona eventually becomes a part of your look and everyone feels comfortable with it. This new awareness of yourself integrates with and becomes part of your ego. Unlike a false self, this is a part of your personality that you had not developed because you did not need it. Once a persona is integrated, it becomes a conscious part of your personality that you can access freely and settle into comfortably.

Some people do not have positive examples to reference. For instance, if a family does not welcome outsiders and the children are taught only to trust and relate to their parents, siblings, and extended family, they may not have the ability to meet strangers and welcome new people into their lives. They may only be able to do this with family members. This type of symbiotic family is generally not open to new people or new ideas. When the rules of behavior do not welcome outsiders, they create a closed family system. If parents do not teach their children how to go out into the world and embrace the unfamiliar, they will need to learn it on their own. For some, shyness and insecurity are barriers to developing this part of their personality.

For many people, change is difficult, even impossible, because they do not want to feel uncomfortable. Yet, uncomfortable feelings are natural and a necessary part of the process of change. In fact, people usually do not make change unless they are uncomfortable. If you feel good, why change? When a person desires to improve herself, she must make it a point to act like that imagined improved self. For example:

> *Carol is a young mother with two children in elementary school and one still at home. Every morning after her two older children go off to school, she joins the neighbors for coffee while the little ones play together. After a few days, Carol realizes that she does not enjoy this time with the neighbors and is bored with their mundane conversation. She decides to enroll her youngest in preschool for three mornings each week and take a class at the university.*
>
> *During the first class, Carol notes that most of the members are well-read and more informed than she is. They*

discuss books she has never heard of, and she learns that their average level of education far exceeds her own. She can see that her vocabulary and life experiences are much different from theirs. She is very uncomfortable at the first meeting, questioning whether she will continue the class.

It will help Carol to know that her awareness of the situation and feelings about it are appropriate. But it is not time for her to cut and run. Rather, it will be in her best interest to acknowledge her discomfort and feelings of inferiority and to acknowledge that she is frightened and intimidated by her classmates. She must accept that her feelings are normal and appropriate and compare her thoughts and assessment of herself to her personal truth. Yes, her classmates are more educated and experienced. Yes, they are well-read. But they have accepted her into the class and she is right where she wants to be. As she continues to study, read, and converse with this group, she will bring herself up to the standard of achievement for which she is striving. She will leave behind the uncomfortable feelings when she achieves her inner goal of self-improvement. These feelings are letting her know that she is stretching herself into becoming the person she imagines she wants to be.

Sometimes a person spends years with a mother or father or spouse who controls everything she does. She learns to act only in response to the controller's expectations and finds her value as a person through pleasing the other. When she is not with her controller and expected to make a decision or present herself to others, she might feel high stress, even panic, because she cannot move smoothly into a supporting persona. She does not know what to do if someone else is not telling her how to behave.

When a person has been married or in a long-term relationship that ends, he may be insecure about meeting a new person. Dating rituals change significantly over ten or fifteen years. A person is often confronted with a changing morality that affects conversation, dress, and sexual expectations. In therapy, the person may admit that he feels anxious about being alone or intimate with another and is afraid of being rejected, just as he felt as a teen. Yet if he realizes that his feelings are normal and appropriate, he will be more likely to allow the discomfort and continue to pursue a new relationship. Eventually his anxiety will subside and he will feel comfortable with this new dimension of his personality.

It is not unusual for someone to sit with me reflecting on their circumstances and feeling depressed because they do not know how to change those circumstances. Years of behaving in one way establishes a pattern of behavior. Breaking away from this pattern is not always easy—in fact, it can be very difficult. You cannot develop a new persona and expand your personality if you cannot envision who you want to be.

You cannot reach a destination unless you have a map directing you to the place you want to go—you will not get to Chicago with a map of Florida. But how do you know who you want to be? To begin, visualize someone that you admire and respect. Since you are looking for an image of a person and not attempting to be someone else, your choice can be a fictional character from a film or a book. It might be someone you have observed but hardly know or someone you know well. It might even be a person that you have imagined or a combination of several personalities. You will choose this imagined person because you see and respect in her those personality traits that are undeveloped in yourself. When you cannot see a desired quality or trait in yourself, you will be attracted to it in someone else. This dynamic is called projection. Imagine how the other would act, dress, or talk in your situation. What kind of gestures, tone of voice, facial expressions, and other cues appeal to you? Practice these before a mirror. Then mimic these mannerisms when you are with others. Remember that if you feel silly or uncomfortable, or others remark that you are acting differently, you are right on course. But, it will not take long before the new behavior is yours; you will feel real in the new role before you know it. Rarely is your discomfort as visible to another as it feels to you. Developing and changing personas is a normal part of personality development. It is important to learn new behaviors in order to adapt to new environments and possibilities.

Rules of behavior

Most of us want to fit in with others. We want to be attracted to others and we want them to find us attractive. We need each other. When people come together in a group, in a family, or in a community, rules or expectations of behavior are established. Members know what others expect of them and they trust one another. Over the course of history humans became a part of civilized communities, and cultures began to develop within those communities. In fact, the definition of the word "civilized" is "to bring a place or people to a stage of social, cultural, and moral development considered to be more advanced." Codes of behavior were meant to bring people together and support all members of the community. Members who did not adhere to the code were ostracized.

These standards of conduct are the basis of what we refer to as manners. Manners result from the standards of conduct that define the best-behaved members, who are moral, educated, cultured, polite, and refined. Manners originally separated civilized from barbaric behavior. They set a standard for human behavior that affords a member of a group social approval. Manners are the measure of normal within the group. However, that which is considered mannerly is susceptible to change due to time, geographical location, and social stratum.

Special occasions often require that we act in ways unique to that occasion. For instance, it is acceptable to whistle and whoop and holler at a baseball game but not at an opera. Nor does it make sense to yell *Bravo!* when our favorite team scores a touchdown. When participating in a toast at a wedding, it is important to know that we must wait until the toast is finished to sip our champagne. Two personal experiences made this clear in my life. On a crowded train in Paris, I realized that people around me avoided eye contact and were not open to conversation. This initially seemed strange to me, but after several minutes I realized that this behavior established boundaries of intimacy with strangers who were sitting very close to one another. These invisible walls created an inner space of privacy, even though they were sitting shoulder to shoulder and thigh to thigh with another's face inches away. Within minutes this practice of manners was important to me as well.

The first time I visited a Buddhist temple, I observed that I was expected to remove my shoes and place them on a shelf with toes pointed out and laces tucked in. It would have been easier to kick them off, I thought, and leave them in a line on the floor. But that would not have respected the established manners and traditions of the place. Understanding how to blend into the established code of honor felt good to me.

That manners matter is evidenced by how much has been written on the subject. Advice columns frequently deal with questions of mannerly behavior, and today training sessions are established solely for the purpose of teaching manners. Some companies and firms sponsor seminars to teach employees and associates mannerly behavior to supplement training in public relations.

A gentleman uses good manners that set him apart from an uncivilized, rude, self-centered, and unpolished man. His gentle manner invites conversation and connection and makes him approachable to others. A lady is courteous and thoughtful of others. She gives to others and makes her environment welcoming. While the terms "lady" and "gentleman" are dated—unless you are beginning a speech—the concept is alive and well among people who are conscious of the way their behavior affects others. Manners take others into consideration and create a peacefulness that allows others to feel comfortable and welcome. Most people learn the elements of mannerly social interaction as young children. However, if someone moves into a new community, she will do better if she learns how to adapt to new expectations. For example:

> *Claire grew up in a small desert town. She speaks in a colloquial small-town manner and is most comfortable in her home environment. When she graduates from high school, she chooses to go to a college in a big city. During her first year, she suffers anxiety and embarrassment because she doesn't have the experience that supports her new environment. She is invited to formal dinners at the homes of her classmates' families and attends sorority events in fine restaurants. She desperately wants to feel comfortable with her new friends and their families. Claire goes to the library and borrows a book on etiquette and manners. While some of the suggestions do not fit her needs, new avenues of understanding open up for her. The next time she is invited to a dinner, a play, or a concert she is able to practice her new social skills. Eventually, as Claire follows a new career in politics, she is comfortable with herself and adopts the protocols that can support her in most situations.*

Rather than back away from social situations that intimidate her, Claire gives herself a makeover. Even though her personality is adequate for her hometown lifestyle, it limits her to that environment. It does not provide her with a broad enough range of behavior for her to feel comfortable as she continues to grow intellectually and socially.

Unexpected life changes

Often in a life journey the road comes to an end, forcing a hard turn to the left or right. You realize that you must completely change direction and it is going to require a reassessment of your role in life. To make wise choices, it is necessary to reflect on your present situation, reset goals, and undertake a decisive course correction. For example:

> *Mark is twenty-four and recently married to Carla. Mark was attracted to Carla's quiet manner and agreeable personality. He considered her a fun companion and good listener. He loved the afternoons they spent together, a welcome quiet time after a full and busy week. But after they have been married for several months, Mark grows tired of staying home all the time. He suggests they meet friends for dinner or invite people over to play cards. Carla is not interested and coaxes Mark to stay home alone with her. She enjoys playing solitaire on her computer, and can lose herself in the game for hours. Mark recognizes that he has three choices: live in the relationship as it is, change it, or leave it. He initiates several conversations, telling her he is feeling suffocated. She empathizes with him and agrees to couple therapy. After several sessions, it becomes clear to Mark and the therapist that Carla has no interest in making any changes. Mark tries for another year to find happiness in his marriage. Carla makes no effort to accommodate his concerns. He finally concludes that he must leave the marriage in order to live the life that is right for him.*

Another example:

Shirley works hard for six years to complete her undergraduate degree in elementary education. She loves to teach and can hardly wait until she has a classroom of her own. Right before the end of her schooling, she begins her student teaching with a master teacher who proves to be a wonderful mentor. After a couple of weeks, Shirley begins to feel stressed. She realizes how difficult it is to manage an over-crowded class of thirty-four students. She spends every night reviewing three papers per student. She has a low tolerance for being in a closed classroom for several hours and feels exhausted at the end of the day with nothing left for her four children at home. She is unavailable to help them with homework and lacks energy for casual conversation with them. She cannot envision herself as a teacher, living this life every day for years. Alarmed that she has spent so much money and time preparing for a career she now doesn't want, Shirley slips into a depression. She is short-tempered and irritable and has lost interest in friends she formerly enjoyed.

After she completes her student teaching, Shirley takes time off to reflect on her life. She sorts out in her mind the parts of teaching that she loves from those she intensely dislikes. She recognizes that she feels confident and exhilarated when she is teaching. On the other hand, she cannot tolerate the restriction of a classroom and believes that much of her time is spent babysitting. She talks with friends and mentors and realizes that she may have chosen the wrong age group. Now recognizing that she does not enjoy spending her time with little children, other than her own, Shirley considers a secondary-school environment. But, upon reflection, this does not appeal to her. She applies to the university to teach a continuing education class and is amazed at the gratification and sense of purpose this new experience affords her. She has found her niche and from then on teaches at the university. Shirley now wakes up every morning looking forward to going to work.

Major changes in lifestyle can cause changes that ripple throughout the family and community, forcing others to change the way they think and behave. To illustrate this, let us take a look at the following couple:

Richard and Tammy have been married for eight years. They are the ideal couple, with two wonderful daughters, a lovely home, and two satisfying careers. They go to church, are well-known for their volunteer work, and are considered a fun couple. It is obvious to everyone who knows them that they love each other and are best friends. Richard and Tammy are the envy of their friends.

One evening Tammy goes to the computer to check her e-mail and finds pornographic sites on the family computer. Horrified, she is most upset because the sites are designed to appeal to a homosexual viewer. Baffled and feeling threatened, she asks herself why her husband would want to go to such sites. She wonders how many times he has done this and whether he is bisexual. What does that even mean? How should she respond to this? The next morning, Tammy tells Richard what she has seen on the computer and asks for an explanation. Richard admits to her that he is confused, assures her of his love for her, and explains that his struggle is in no way caused by her. He explains that he has been drawn to homosexuality for years, has not discussed it with anyone, and knows he is gay. He tells her of his struggle between his love for her and his complete disinterest in their sex life. Sex between them has been infrequent throughout their marriage; friendship and their relationship with their daughters have replaced sexual intimacy. Richard admits that he has been spending time with a man and leading a double life. Tammy and Richard spend a weekend talking about homosexuality, the lack of intimacy in their marriage, and their confused feelings.

On Monday Tammy calls me for a therapy appointment. She wants someone to talk with who is knowledgeable about marital relationships and who will not make a moral judgment about her husband. She believes her life is falling apart and wants to find some way to save her marriage. She cannot envision where she and Richard are heading and is terrified, wondering how all of this might impact their children and their family life.

This couple spends many therapy sessions in conversation and tears. Their relationship with each other and the future they had envisioned for their children has changed. As they continue in therapy, other truths surface that they have been ignoring. Tammy has gained one hundred pounds since their wedding day. She insists that Richard is her best friend but is not sure how she should feel about a husband. She loves the fun they have and the time they spend together, but she does not feel sexual. She also reveals that her extended family includes several gay men who have never come out. She wonders what their lives have been like. She feels like a pioneer going into new and frightening territory without a map or guide.

Richard is terrified that he will be shamed and excluded from their extended family, all of whom are people of faith. He believes that everyone in the family sees homosexuality as unnatural and a matter of choice. How can he ever live a gay lifestyle and still parent his children and stay connected to his wife and family? Whatever decisions Richard makes will call for a drastic change in his lifestyle. Everyone in his life will be affected. If he embraces his homosexuality, he will lose his marriage, his relationship with his children will change, and he may be cut off from his family. Richard is unsure of what coming out will mean to his coworkers, and he feels threatened about his work.

If Richard does not come out, he will continue to live a double life and never be honest with himself. A good solution can only result from extensive conversation with those most intimately involved. A decision will be a reflection of the truth and goodness that comes out of these dialogues. Both Richard and Tammy must work closely with a guide who will be their truth speaker and help them walk through the muck of this change.

Many are affected by such lifestyle changes and many get through them. More often than not their lives continue in a good way. When a person makes drastic changes in lifestyle in order to live out his own truth, he will find the transition easier when he realizes that he has chosen his behavior in response to his needs and not the feelings of others. His feelings are the result of his relationship to his own truth. His personal truth is formed by beliefs that come from sorting out and interpreting his own perception of his environment or circumstances. When he comes to a decision that supports his personal truth, he will experience peace within himself. In order to live his truth, he may eventually need to distance himself from the anger and derision of others who have a different truth and different expectations of him.

The vignette above will draw multiple responses from you, the reader. Each person will come to some thought or decision based on their personal background and experiences and their religious training. Each will have their own idea of what Richard and Tammy should do. We can imagine the reactions and responses of relatives and acquaintances. But, in the end, how this situation is addressed must be decided by each person involved. Many will try to change Richard's and Tammy's minds. Others will question their own perceptions and beliefs in order to maintain a relationship with the couple. And others will walk away from them, unable to handle the tension of a family member living a lifestyle that is not acceptable to them. Yet, in the end, Tammy and Richard, like the rest of us, must choose to live the best life they can. They cannot live a life that is unacceptable to them in order to please others.

Today I encounter more harmonious solutions to serious life change than I did twenty years ago. I see more couples who can go through a divorce and remain kind and respectful to each other, because they want to be kind and respectful people. I see more couples who maintain a workable, even enjoyable, relationship with each other after one spouse comes out and embraces his homosexuality. Families are establishing new positions for members in their extended families. Former husbands and wives can be introduced as: *My friend, Joe, the father of my children* or *Joe is my former husband* or *This is Mary, the mother of my children. She and Jean are partners.* Some can say, *This is Tom; he and I were married for many years.* I see that some people are willing to drop the hateful and hurtful judgments and comments as they learn that everyone needs to make personal choices based in their personal truth and not the personal biases of others.

Living a responsible, conscientious lifestyle is not selfish, and it is not the same as doing anything you want. Rather, a responsible life is one that is true to you, but does not endanger or impede the rights of another. It is a lifestyle lived in response to your personal moral code. You have the opportunity to interact with many people in your life, exchanging moral views and ideas. From this interaction with others, you will develop your own sense of right and wrong, which allows you to interact with others peacefully. You do not need everyone's approval, not that you would ever get it anyway. You must find a way to live with those closest to you. We are all responsible for taking care of our children and those who depend on us. But, your lifestyle should also take care of you and be enjoyable. This is not selfishness.

Points to remember about developing a personal behavior style:

- You are not who others say you are, nor are you limited to the expectations of others.
- Life is like a drama in which you are the star. How well you play your part will help to determine how the story will unfold.
- You make an infinite number of choices in determining who you will be and how you will live your life.
- If you live a life that does not reflect your personal truth, you are at risk for symptoms of anxiety or depression.
- When you come to a decision that supports your personal truth, you will experience peace within yourself.
- A mature person can allow others to make life decisions and life changes that differ from what she thinks is right. A mature person realizes that everyone must make choices that agree with her own moral compass.
- Developing a persona is a healthy way to make change and adapt to a new environment.
- People are more likely to make changes when they are uncomfortable.
- People tend to create patterns of behavior. Interrupting or changing a behavior pattern can be difficult. It takes intention and hard work.
- Community codes of behavior and standards of conduct are the basis of what we refer to as manners.

- Manners take others into consideration and create a peacefulness that allows others to feel comfortable and welcome.
- Major changes in lifestyle cause changes that ripple throughout the family and community, challenging others to change the way they think and behave.

Chapter 7

Assertive Behavior

Assertive behavior promotes equality in human relationships, enabling us to act in our own best interests, to stand up for ourselves without undue anxiety, to express feelings honestly and comfortably, to exercise personal rights without denying the rights of others.

Robert E. Alberti and Michael L. Emmons, from
Your Perfect Right: Assertiveness and Equality in Your Life and Relationships

Be true to yourself and others

Like so many others, I was exposed to the idea of being assertive in the early 1960s. Leadership classes, psychotherapy sessions, and personal growth seminars drew from the energy of the women's movement, stressing the importance of a woman finding her voice and discovering her potential. Modern women writers ignited the energy of young women and encouraged them to examine their lives and expand their choices. These messages touched not only the hearts of women but many fathers, husbands, sons, and brothers as well. I was a child of the 1940s and 1950s. I did not personally respond to this new voice until the1970s, when the awareness that I could become my own woman, develop my gifts and talents, and make choices and decisions that would work for me as well as my family became a personal epiphany. I had quickly grasped the concept of assertiveness, but it took years for me to integrate the behavior into my personality.

To help you learn to assert yourself, I suggest a posture that I always encourage my clients to assume: *This is who I am, this is what I want, and this is how I want to be treated.* At this point the work gets sluggish. I have found that most people do not know what they want. They are quick to explain what they do *not* want but not what they *do* want. For instance, I commonly hear statements like this: *I don't want to be like my mother* or *I don't want to be such a bitch anymore* or *I don't want people to walk over me anymore.* These statements will not be helpful to you. It is as if you are planning a journey and I ask you: *Where do you want to go?* It will not be useful if you tell me where you do not want to go. You must have a destination. You must flip those initial statements so they look more like: *I want to be different than my mother, I want to be . . .* or *I want to learn to stay calm when I'm stressed and control my anger* or *I want to start standing up for myself.* These statements point you in the right direction toward the person you are and the person you want to be. You must begin the change by looking to yourself, not to others. In previous chapters, you have learned how to discover the real you. Now, you will learn how to act like the real you.

You must decide how you want to be treated. You must tell others what you want. You must insist that others treat you well. Let's look at one way Bentley has learned to assert himself:

> *Bentley resents that his wife, Allison, ridicules him and often teases him in a mocking way. She chides him in front of their children. He tries to ignore his wife's behavior, but eventually he loses his temper and either yells at her, which ends in an argument, or he leaves the house. Bentley does not like any of this and wonders how his children really feel about him. He reflects on his behavior and asks himself whether he actually does act like a child; he decides that he does not. He makes a decision to talk with his wife*

about this dynamic. He waits until the two of them are in a quiet, peaceful mood, and they have the following conversation:

Bentley: *I would like to talk with you about something that happened this morning. Do you have a minute to listen? I am irritated by the way you treated me. I think you often talk to me in a ridiculing way. Maybe you are teasing, but it is hurtful and I don't like it. I would like you to stop doing this. I am not a fool, and I think your way of speaking makes me look like one in front of our children.*

Allison: *I don't know what you're talking about. I'm teasing—can't you take a joke? You know I love you, and the kids do too.*

Bentley: *Loving me is not the point. I believe you and the kids love me, but I don't like the way you talk down to me and laugh at me. I am an intelligent adult. But I think your tone is mocking and demeaning. I do not want our children to learn to talk that way to me or to anyone else.*

Allison: *I think you're making too much of this; I don't really know what you're talking about.*

Bentley: *I just wanted to tell you this, and the next time you are doing it, I will stop you and let you know you are doing it again.*

The next time it happened, Bentley did interrupt his wife. He pointed out that she was again ridiculing him and he asked her to rephrase her words. His wife reflected on what he had said to her, and she gradually stopped this annoying and hurtful habit.

Notice that Bentley interrupted Allison while she was repeating her negative behavior in front of the children. Some might disagree that this discussion should take place with the children present, and often couples are counseled not to confront each other in front of their children. But this is an important teaching time for them. They have witnessed the negative behavior, so it is best that the positive behavior be presented in front of them as well.

It is important for children to learn assertiveness, and not aggression, as modeled by their parents. They will benefit from Bentley's confronting the behavior (not Allison personally, but her behavior) and hearing their mother's proper response. They will benefit from observing the manner in which their father facilitated the change in her behavior. They will also learn that inappropriate behavior is not acceptable with people outside of their family, and this will help them not to imitate the poor behavior. Children too often see their parents' negative behavior while rarely observing an appropriate confrontation and its ultimate resolution.

Remember that children are always observing their parents and need to learn how to express their needs to others. Children do not benefit from parents' arguments, fights, name-calling, and other hurtful behavior. But they benefit for a lifetime when they hear: *I don't like to be treated this way* or *I'm sorry for the way I acted, you don't deserve that* or *I'm sorry that hurt you, I won't do it again.* Parents become heroes to their children when they can also speak this way to them: *I'm sorry for yelling at you; you don't deserve to be yelled at* or *I'm sorry for what I said to you; I wish I had not said it.*

Assertive people are kind

Kindness is an essential element of assertive behavior. Assertive people are careful to treat others in a respectful way, and they make the effort to learn kind ways to disagree with others and tell them what they need and want. No good reasons exist to be hurtful to another person. Assertive people communicate well with others, explaining their actions without being defensive. They understand that others have questions and doubts and know they cannot take away hurtful feelings for the other. But what they can do is ease the concerns of others by treating them with dignity. When they think their assertiveness might be too direct for others, they are able to temper their actions without selling themselves short. Assertive people are never mean.

To better understand assertive behavior, let us look at it in relation to three types of behavior: passive, passive-aggressive, and aggressive.

Passive behavior

Passive people may worry about hurting the feelings of another and fear the reaction of others. They are submissive and leave themselves powerless in their interactions with others. The passive person does not hold herself in high esteem. She believes that she is weaker, less important and less valuable than others. Her words, actions, and demeanor tell those around her that she is unworthy of their attention or recognition. A passive person may have difficulty joining new groups of people, asking for a promotion, representing herself well, or recognizing her own talents and strengths. Passive people may not know how to accept praise or compliments and try to avoid them altogether. They often turn praise into a compliment for the other, for example: *You're too good to me* or *You're so nice* or *I'll never do it as well as you.* It is difficult for them to say, *Yes, I feel good about the way it turned out, and thank you for noticing.*

Passive people often do not tell others what they want. Because they feel unworthy of attention, love, or the benefits of a friendship, they do not allow themselves to take or enjoy what they could have. In passive and emotionally unhealthy ways, people sometimes do things or behave in a manner that they detest, in order to be accepted. Sometimes, people do not act at all, because they do not want to be noticed, praised, or blamed.

In therapy, Ida identified her strongly passive behavior:

> *I am so lonely since my husband and I retired. He likes to stay around the house and work on the computer. He is in touch with friends that he knew in the service. They always exchange stories and jokes. I didn't know those guys, so it doesn't interest me that much. I've thought I might go to a yoga class or start a pinochle group. But Sam likes me to be home. He likes his lunch ready at noon and then we take a nap. I like to read and I like being with Sam. He and I do go out often, but we're always together. I would like to go out alone more often. I meet with some of the women I used to work with, but they are all younger and I don't have anything in common with them anymore. I want to meet some new people. I think Sam will be hurt if I tell him I want to go out alone two or three mornings or afternoons a week. I don't want him to think I don't want to be with him.*

Clearly, Ida is concerned about and thoughtful of Sam. She wants to take his needs into consideration, and everything she is doing for him is good. However, she is not doing anything for herself. She has put all her social needs aside in her concern for Sam's desires. She is in a less than equal relationship, but she has put herself there. I have found that this common situation occurs because the passive person assumes the subordinate role without the other ever realizing his partner wants anything to be different. The fear that keeps her from asserting herself is rooted in irrational beliefs she has about herself and perhaps about Sam. Often, when the passive person shares her loneliness with her partner, he is willing to help with a more equitable schedule. He very likely believes that she is as happy as he is, and she has not been telling him anything different.

Perhaps Ida fears that Sam will become abusive. Maybe he has a history of abusive behavior. If this is true, Ida must still confront the problem. In this instance, she will surely benefit from some professional assistance like couples counseling. To have a healthy relationship with Sam and alleviate her loneliness, she must learn to assert herself. When a passive person learns early in life the lie that she does not have value (or has less value than others), she may spend the rest of her life in a passive, or victim, role.

A passive person might not trust herself enough to make a decision and simply chooses what she assumes the other wants, not even asking herself what she wants. Or she may deny her own needs when confronted by the other. For example, one day a woman called me and in a quiet, meek voice inquired about an assertiveness training class she had heard I was planning. After speaking to her for some time, she registered for the class. Before she hung up the phone, she told me how excited she was about the class. Later that afternoon, her husband called to say: *She won't be attending your class, she's assertive enough.* I did not hear from the woman again. Unfortunately, this dynamic is not uncommon. The passive person allows someone else to make her decisions and decide what is good for her.

Aggressive behavior

Aggressive behavior is about power and control. The aggressive person must feel in control of his situation and he assumes this power by controlling others. He does not adapt well to the needs and concerns of others, unless they align with his. When there is a disruption or a disagreement, he uses power and force to get his way. He gets his needs met by intimidating, or bullying, the other to comply with his wishes. He will use threats of physical or verbal abuse to overpower the other. He induces fear in the other until his needs or wants are met. He places his needs and wants before those of others, and he does not care to know or meet their needs. In the example above, the husband aggressively canceled his wife's assertiveness training. He did not consider her needs or wants. He used bullying behavior to cancel the class and overpower her interest in self-improvement.

Underlying aggressive behavior is a deep sense of inferiority. The aggressive person is afraid that his needs will not get met if he does not demand specific responses from others. He actually feels out of control and maintains the status quo by forcing others to comply with his ideas of comfort and security. If another person makes a decision or detours from his plan, he feels threatened and out of control. Imagine what would happen to the husband mentioned above if his wife took assertiveness training. He might lose control of her, she might disagree with him, and in his worst possible scenario, she might leave him. Being out of control is terrifying to an aggressive person who must control a situation by controlling others.

Consider how Art handles his role as a father:

Art's sixteen-year-old son attends a dance with friends. He decides to drive a friend home because his friend's parent could not leave work to pick him up as planned. Art becomes concerned when his son does not come home at the time he is expected. Art begins to rave about his worthless son and his disrespect for the rules of the family. He gets in his car and goes to the home of his son's friend. Once there he pounds on the door, demanding that

> *his son* Come out here right now. *When they return home, Art berates him until the teen is crying. Art screams at him:* You don't have to like me, but you will respect me.

You be the therapist. What is wrong here? First, Art has no respect for his son's ability to address a problem. He does not value his son's perception of the problem and cares not at all that his son has made a kind gesture in assuring that his friend gets home safely. He talks to his son in a demeaning and bullying way, using fear, and demands to get him to do what he wants. And Art demands that his son respect him. Most of us realize respect is something that is earned and learned from example and not demanded of someone. Art's son learns that his father is out of control, cannot be trusted, is not the one to turn to for assurance or advice, and that he is certainly not a positive role model. Art does not earn his son's respect.

Another way Art could have faced the situation is to acknowledge his fear for his son's safety: *Where is my son? He is later than I expected. I hope he is OK.* When he got to the friend's home, he might have rung the doorbell and waited for someone to come. Then he could have described his concern and asked for information. Once he located his son, a better way to have greeted him would have been: *I've been so worried. Are you all right?* Then he needed to listen to his son. How did he feel? What was his perception of the evening? How could he praise his son for his compassion and good decision-making? When a parent does not know where his child is and is worrying that he might be harmed, he feels powerless and realizes he has no control over the situation. But being out of control is a fact of life. None of us are really ever completely in control of anything. But assuming control through bullying and abuse does not help one to gain control either. A better response would have been one of kindness and acceptance. Art's son would have respected him for this response and he would have been more likely to come to him for advice or assurance in the future.

So what is the difference between an aggressive bully and a sociopath? The aggressive bully may in fact be sociopathic. But there is a good chance he is not. If he had a parent figure who was a bully (or a sociopath), he most likely never learned how to manage his fear and insecurities. Bullying and force is the behavior he has learned to use to express his fear. He can learn to identify his fears and express them in another way. Then he can choose an appropriate behavior. A sociopath has no capacity to feel concern for the other. Therefore, he has no motivation to choose a behavior that will show concern and caring. We cannot expect him to change and we are wise to expect bullying and aggression or passive-aggressive behavior from him.

Be aware that a healthy level of aggressiveness exists that allows one to take control of a situation and direct or lead others to a positive end point. When a police officer instructs people to move away from a dangerous area, he must be aggressive to get the attention of those involved and to give directions. At your place of work, you will note that those who aggressively overcome obstacles to their goals generally accomplish those goals quickly. Anyone who depends on producing or selling a product must address their market aggressively and with enthusiasm. This type of aggressive behavior is not the same as that which seeks to control and use others in a hurtful or demeaning manner.

Passive-aggressive behavior

Passive behavior can have a more sinister look. Like the aggressive person, the passive person has a poor self-image and thinks she is powerless. She does not know what to do with her hurtful feelings that cause her anger, feelings like disappointment, fear, jealousy, or guilt. She believes her bad feelings are caused by others, and she needs to punish them for making her feel as she does. So that others will like and accept her, or not notice her at all, she does not let them know what she does. Her actions are aggressive, but hidden by a nice or benign façade. Or they go completely unnoticed. For example:

> *Pam works in a large medical facility where she supervises several nurses. She gets along with her staff and they work well together, except for one person. Jean is fun and outgoing and does not take long to make friends with everyone. Soon the others are asking her for advice and sharing experiences with her. Pam is more reserved and quiet, and she becomes jealous of Jean. She feels excluded because the others easily make plans with Jean to do things outside of work. Sometimes they include Pam and sometimes they do not. Pam becomes suspicious, wondering,* Is Jean trying to take over? Does she want my job? Has Jean taken my place with my friends? *Eventually Pam becomes angry because she has to work daily with Jean. She is jealous because Jean laughs so much with her friends and because Jean does a good job and is respected. Pam does not know how to stop feeling angry.*

The passive-aggressive person often looks like a nice person to others. She wants to please them, or look good to them, so she does not let herself reveal negative feelings. She does not know how to express anger appropriately, and she does not know what do with her disappointments or feelings of jealousy. Instead she is secretive about the way she gets back at others. Passive-aggressive behavior is often chosen as a way to punish someone or to hurt them in some way.

The passive-aggressive person does not know how, or is afraid, to tell others what she feels. Rather than express her feelings of disappointment or anger, she assumes the other should know what she feels or wants and punishes him for not caring about her. But he may not expect the punishment and may not know that she is hurt or angry or what the reasoning is behind those feelings. It is unfair to expect him to guess what she needs or to read her mind. Large family gatherings like holidays, weddings, and funerals can spark hurtful feelings that nobody will talk about. This explains why so many of these gatherings end with even more hurt feelings. It also reveals why family members do not speak to one another and why these feuds sometimes continue for decades.

Passive-aggressive behavior is interrupted when the passive-aggressive person is expected to tell her feelings and relate exactly what she thinks makes her feel as she does. When others will not buy her story of what someone did to her, her behavior loses its power and she is exposed. She must be encouraged to own her feelings and learn an appropriate way to talk about them, before she can be assertive. As she recovers from this crippling behavior, she will learn that it is normal for her to feel angry, jealous, disappointed, and afraid. She will learn to identify and express these hurtful feelings. When she recognizes them as her own, she will be able to express them and interpret them. Once she can do this, she will feel better and not need to secretly attack the other person.

Gossip is an age-old and excellent example of passive-aggressive behavior. More is said about this in Chapter 11. In its most extreme form, passive-aggressiveness, like aggressive behavior, can look like sociopathic behavior because it is mean-spirited. Again, the difference is the ability of the person to be aware of and care about the needs of the other. The passive-aggressive person has not learned how to accept her feelings and choose appropriate behavior. The sociopath does not have the capacity to care for the other, and he will never learn genuine appropriate behavior.

Before you can attain a mature, assertive communication style, it is essential to learn assertive behavior. If your primary way of behaving is to be passive, if you are waiting to see how the world will treat you, your communication style will follow suit. The way you communicate will announce that you are powerless and you are looking for someone to take control. And, trust me, there is always someone who will take control of you. If your primary way of behaving is aggressive, or taking control of others, your style of communication will tell others that about you. You will likely attract someone who is passive and you will be able to control, or bully, them.

But you will be frustrated in your attempt to control a person who makes her own decisions. If you do not feel empowered and you believe that others must approve of everything you do, you might find some inappropriate or self-destructive behavior to make you feel better about yourself; or you might develop some negative, nasty way of treating others with whom you are angry.

Remember that not one of us fits into a defined slot that will describe us accurately. This chapter is about behavior and not about actual people. All of us have the potential to behave in all of the ways described above. And an infinite array and blend of these behaviors exist. Some are more prominent in us, and it is important to identify our assertive, passive, and aggressive behaviors to help us make our best choices. You will learn in Part II of this book that your ability to communicate will reflect the person you want to be—the New You.

Points to remember about assertive and non-assertive behavior:

- The assertive person lets others know who she is, what she wants, and how she wants to be treated.
- The assertive person emphasizes what she prefers rather than what she doesn't like.
- Children learn to be assertive by modeling parents' assertive behavior.
- Kindness and respect for self and others are the basis of assertiveness.
- Assertive communication is direct, firm, clear, and kind.
- Passive behavior stems from feelings of fear and poor self-worth.
- The passive person shies away from taking personal responsibility. Her style of communication is indirect and unclear.
- A deep sense of inferiority underlies aggressive behavior.
- The aggressive person must control every situation and only feels powerful when controlling others. He often uses power and force to get his way. He typically gets his needs met by intimidating or bullying others into complying with his wishes.
- An angry and aggressive person's communication style disrespects others and is unkind.
- Healthy aggressiveness allows one to take control of a situation and direct or lead others to a positive end point.
- Like the aggressive person, the passive-aggressive person does not know what to do with the hurtful feelings that cause her anger.
- It is important for the passive-aggressive person to be accepted by others (or not to stand out), so her aggression

takes place in secret. It is important to her that her mean behavior not be traced back to her.

- The passive-aggressive person's actions are aggressive, although her aggression is hidden by an innocent or benign facade.
- The passive-aggressive person's communication style is indirect, unclear, and hurtful.

Chapter 8

Deepening Awareness

I lose my center. I feel dispersed, scattered, in pieces. I must have time alone in which to mull over any encounter and to extract its juice, its essence, to understand what has really happened to me as a consequence of it.

May Sarton, American writer

The soul

For many years I have sought to learn about the soul. Countless definitions and theories exist about the nature of the soul. Every culture, religion, and era has a commentary about it. Theologians, philosophers, and psychologists have debated its existence and nature for millennia. Although the belief is pervasive that humans have souls, a definition that all can agree on remains elusive. I do not want to enter into a debate or attempt to convert you to any particular belief. You have some idea of what you believe and what you do not, and many wonderful resources are available to help you explore the nature of the soul with integrity.

My aim is to tell you what I believe and the ways in which I experience the soul in my personal life and in my work. I think it will enrich this discussion if you reflect on your experiences and beliefs and see where we agree and where our views diverge.

Definition of soul

Historically, the mysteries of physical life were explained by the presence of unseen spirits. Early humans explained that everything from thunder and lightning to natural disasters to the mysteries surrounding conception, birth, and death were caused by the interference of good and evil spirits and gods and goddesses.

Today, scientific discovery provides reasonable theories that help us to understand the countless ways in which life germinates and the different paths that life takes until death. We understand that natural changes in the earth, ocean currents, and atmosphere can produce catastrophes like earthquakes, tsunamis, and famine. We know these events as *Acts of God.* We understand that the earth is continually changing. It was not created in six days but has been evolving over billions of years. We have learned that the universe is expanding and that the earth is not at its center. As our rational minds interpret old myths we understand more about creation, but we still do not know or understand the ultimate source of creation, death, and rebirth. We connect to this mystery of the unknown as if it were godly or divine.

This mystery is what humans have assigned names to born of their culture, names like *Yahweh*, *Allah*, *Zeus*, *Jupiter*, and *Heavenly Father.* Recent popular names for this mystery are *the Universe, the Source,* and *A Higher Power*. This divine source is the organizing principle and the essence of all forms of life in our universe and beyond. It is the heartbeat, the summation, and the source of all of creation and what I know as God. When my actions, intentions, and emotions are in alignment with God or the natural order of things, I am content and feel in harmony with nature and the people around me. I believe that God is that essence within me and all others, whether or not we choose to name this higher power or believe in it. The mystery of creation, life, death, and beyond is essential to being human. This essence of God is what I identify as the soul in me. Words such as "sacred," "holy," "whole," and "divine love" describe the soul for me.

It is often said that "the eyes are the window of the soul." Many people believe that animals have souls; I believe they do. My belief is supported when I look into my cockapoo's eyes and see pure, unconditional love. I have seen her concern for me and her fear when she thinks I am threatened by someone coming to the door or approaching me when we are walking together. I see this in my pet just as I see it in people.

Eyes tell me when something is not right with others. I have observed clients suffering from brain disorders, depression, drug addiction, and anorexia. Their eyes seem to be crying out: *Help me, I'm dying,* even though their words may be telling me they had a great week. I've seen the look of death in a client's eyes when a situation in their life seems to be killing them. This is not uncommon when someone is in a hopeless marriage or going through a vicious divorce process. It is obvious to me when a person is feeling hopeless. It is as if their soul is dying.

I have had personal experience with the *look of death.* I once lay very sick from a ruptured appendix in an emergency room waiting for a surgeon. My husband and a friend were at my side. Later, my friend said she had thought I was going to die before the surgeon arrived. When I asked why she thought this, she replied that my eyes were telling her that I was leaving my body. My doctor later confirmed her observation when he diagnosed the severity of my condition.

I have observed the dull expression in the eyes of sociopaths who lack emotion and connection. While he is telling me of his good intentions and his love for his wife or girlfriend and children, his eyes are saying nothing. When we have natural eye contact with someone we can see their fear and loneliness or sadness. We can also clearly see their joy and enthusiasm. When someone is describing what he loves—his wife, children, home, or passion—his eyes light up, and you can see something within him come to life.

The soul is the difference between *having sex* and *making love*. Two people make a physical connection through having sex. But when making love, two people share intimacy and enter into a communion or deeper life connection. They are truly spiritually and emotionally naked and accepting of one another. When a couple makes love, they are entering into an expectation of a relationship and the possibility of a shared life. Looking into the eyes of a lover can connect two people to something wonderful that is greater than both of them. The great thirteenth-century Persian spiritual poet Rumi speaks of such a union:

A moment of happiness,
you and I sitting on the verandah,
apparently two, but one in soul, you and I.
We feel the flowing water of life here,
you and I, with the garden's beauty
and the birds singing.
The stars will be watching us,
and we will show them
what it is to be a thin crescent moon.
You and I unselfed, will be together,
indifferent to idle speculation, you and I.
The parrots of heaven will be cracking sugar
as we laugh together, you and I.
In one form upon this earth,
and in another form in a timeless sweet land.

To make art something must happen consciously through the ego: *I made this* or *I composed this.* But when creativity comes from the soul, it finds its own way. It becomes something the ego (See sidebar, p. xx) had not planned and did not know it could do. Michelangelo, arguably the greatest sculptor of all time, said he did not plan his beautiful works of art; instead he released the forms trapped in the stone. The images originated in his imagination but took on their own definition as he chiseled the stone. Something other than his conscious thought brought the images into existence and created his masterpieces. We can learn from this if we take care not to let the fearful messages of the ego overpower our experience: *I can't draw, or dance, or sing* or *Whatever I create turns out badly.* Let your painting, or music, or dance flow. Tell yourself: *I don't need to know what it is as I'm doing it; I can see what it is when it is finished.* Turn on the music or pick up a paintbrush and give expression to your imagination. See what comes from your soul.

A gifted storyteller pulls the listener in until she feels like one of the characters in the story. The feeling lingers after the book is closed or the story is finished, and the reader or listener continues to think about the characters or the story line. We enter into the story because it touches something deep within us. Great music and dance bring audiences to tears and tell a story, even when no words are spoken. We go to museums because the art captures our soul, pulling us in with a sense of wonder and awe. Art is a vehicle through which the soul expresses itself when words and rational thought are inadequate. Visitors to museums must sit with a piece of art and allow it to fill them. What is felt from the soul cannot be explained rationally, just as one cannot accurately describe a baby's smile or the look in a lover's eye.

Dreams and imagination are the language of the soul. Both speak in a discursive, nonlinear way, and the images move from one focus to another with no attention to logic. Have you climbed

The Importance of Sleep

Sleep is essential for optimum physical, emotional, and spiritual health. The National Sleep Association recommends eight to ten hours of sleep a day. When we are sleep-deprived or our sleep is sporadic, our circadian rhythm* is interrupted, affecting mood, concentration, attention span, and personal relationships. Many studies, easily found online, compare sleep deprivation to intoxication. Sufficient sleep during a twenty-four-hour span allows for time to play and work, to spend time with friends and family, and to go outside and exercise.

* *A circadian rhythm is a biological process that is adjusted by external cues such as daylight or temperature, and it moderates our sleep cycle.*

the side of a building or felt yourself flying without wings in your dreams? Dreams use the language of archetypal, or classic, symbols and images that the brain organizes into a story. Like biblical parables, dreams use metaphor to convey a message to the dreamer through drama and story. The message is deeper than the ego can easily recognize, since the ego's way of understanding is to make sense of things, to order thought in a recognizable pattern. To understand and interpret a dream, one must learn the language of images. People have an average of five cycles of dreaming in a good night's sleep. In order to accomplish this, the dreamer needs sufficient sleep.

We give voice to the soul through spiritual disciplines such as prayer, meditation, contemplation, and other spiritual practice. Each of us must find the practice that allows us to quiet our minds and open ourselves to the depths of our souls. Most likely you will not have an immediate moment of epiphany. But at a later time you may come to a new awareness and say to yourself: *Where did that come from?*

Spiritual practices like meditation are believed to nurture the soul and lead to self-realization, or wholeness, and ultimately to a closer union with God. I am confident that we are united with God through our soul and through our souls we are connected with one another. I think quietly listening to music or daydreaming is similar to meditation.

I believe moments exist in our lives when we are overcome by a sense of awe and wonder. These moments can be breathtaking and beyond description. They may be impossible to convey to another, unless that person has had a similar experience (in which case words are unnecessary). Such moments make the ordinary *extraordinary* and often evoke an emotional response.

As a young woman, following the birth of my son, I had a near-death experience. I felt myself leaving my body, although I was fully conscious. I felt indescribably peaceful and filled with wonder. My mind said: *So this is what dying is like?* I was not concerned that I had not yet held my newborn or that I had another son waiting for me at home. I was in a different, mystical place of incredible peace.

I recall this experience as, *An awareness that everything was as it is meant to be.* I had a conscious awareness that I was dying, yet I felt no accompanying fear. I knew that although my physical self was dying, it was not going to be the end of me. The word*s* that came to me were "going toward." I had no idea where I was going, but I was certain it was not my end—I was going toward something big. This experience did not include any religious thoughts or images, but it left me with a deeper spiritual awareness that there is more to me than my body. I can reflect on the feeling of this moment but have never been able to describe it accurately. After that experience, I have never again feared death.

Often those present at the birth of a baby are touched and tearful, even the medical staff for whom childbirth is routine. I was taken by surprise when my first grandson was born. Minutes after he came into this world, I looked into his eyes and he gazed back at me, grasping my finger. My eyes filled with tears and I felt deeply connected to something indescribably bigger than both of us. Perhaps this is an archetypal experience of mothers and grandmothers since the beginning of time. One time when I was in a hospital waiting room, I observed a six-foot-tall, three-hundred-pound new father holding his baby daughter for the first time. He enfolded the five-pound infant in the crook of his elbow while covering her entire body with his other hand. Tears were running down his face, and I, too, was moved to tears at the beauty and tenderness of this sight. This man was a stranger to me, yet for a few minutes his love for his tiny daughter touched my soul.

The moments spent with a friend or family member as they begin the dying process are often soul stirring. To be with the dying as they move in and out of consciousness is an intimate and very personal time. My husband, John, who has prayed with many at their deaths, both as a former priest and a hospice bereavement counselor, describes his response to the mystery of death: *I feel a profound sense of wonder. What is really happening for this person, I ask myself, knowing that their experience will someday be mine.* I wonder whether the discomfort of the observer, so common in the family and friends of the dying, comes from the ego's overwhelming fear of death. Still, this fear can be transformed by the manifestation of the soul at this time.

The feeling of the soul comes over us at special times, but also in ordinary moments. Many years ago I was downhill skiing in Utah, and while riding the chairlift, it stopped high in midair. A profound silence prevailed on the mountain, enveloping me. Twenty feet away rose an enormous pine, its icicles hanging down like twinkling crystals on a chandelier. The branches of the tree moved so slightly I almost missed the movement. The icicles tinkled, making a breathtaking musical sound, yet I could not detect a breeze. Overcome with wonder, I thought with amazement how this tree had stood in this place for decades and now chose to speak to me, a witness to its magnificent display of beauty.

Later that afternoon, when I skied down to the lodge and met my friends, I tried to explain what had happened to me. My friends were underwhelmed. One said to me: *Wow, Patty, you saw a pine tree with icicles? You live a sheltered life.* We both laughed.

I experience a feeling of the soul when camping in the desert and I look up at the stars. A mysterious pull from above connects me to something much grander than myself, something that touches me deeply. I experience this at the beach while gazing at the water and listening to the surf. When a client has shared deep suffering and pain or immense joy, I am drawn into their story and feel an instantaneous sense of connection. I do not always anticipate when I will feel or experience the soul. My mind cannot predict or plan these serendipitous experiences. They just happen.

The goal of psychotherapy is *to gain a sense of understanding life at a new level of peacefulness and self-acceptance.* Psychotherapy is not a good experience if someone uses it to complain about others and enter into a self-destructive pattern of doom and gloom. The role of the therapist is to lead the client to a sense of wholeness, to an integration of his soul or spirit, body, and mind. Someone does not get this from merely memorizing catchy pop-psychology phrases. It comes from making a space in our lives for the goodness within us to become conscious, and we must allow this goodness to ease the guilt that overshadows our bad behavior. The soul quiets and overwrites the shame and fear of the ego. It offers new ways of being and of understanding our life experiences.

We have historically looked to religious experience to feel the presence of God. Too often religions miss the mark and function at an ego level, more concerned with righteous rules and boundaries, allowing little space for the soul to manifest. At its best, religion directs one's focus to God, and at its worst, it is egoistic and competitive as each religion strives to be the best and only true one. The leaders of these religions, like many heads of states and monarchs from the Dark Ages until today, are honored as gods or messengers of God, and they impose rules that are self-serving and divisive.

The purpose of religion is to direct our attention to God. But we must distinguish religion and its doctrines and dogmas and traditions from God, or we may miss the experience of God. An ancient Buddhist story provides an engaging metaphor:

> *Truth has nothing to do with words. Truth can be likened to the bright moon in the sky. Words, in this case, can be likened to a finger. The finger can point to the moon. However, to see the moon, one must gaze beyond the finger.*

The soul is not contained or directed by rules, moral codes, or laws. Such dictums are necessary for the ego to feel safe and protected, but the soul flows freely. The soul is not concerned with religion, monuments, or authority. The soul is only concerned with wholeness and holiness and with the integration of soul and spirit, body and mind. When we are at peace, physically well, and not deluged with worry and fear, we feel balance. Our lives run smoother and we have the time and energy to be compassionate with others and at peace with ourselves.

In working with individuals who are traumatized or living in depression and anxiety, I have learned that unresolved conflicts dictate their lives. They might be obsessive in recalling painful events from the past or in anticipating what might happen in the future. This fearful activity of the ego must be quieted to allow the serenity of the soul to be felt and for healing to begin. I often ask: *What are you doing in your life that is not right for you?* or *What are you not doing with your life that you need to do?* After reflection, the answer can lead to the cure.

At times when there is no good resolution to a situation and emotional pain continues, pathos, or suffering, can consume one emotionally and suck out the very breath of life. Sometimes people experience something so horrible they feel—and often look—as if their soul is dying. Talk therapy cannot be the only choice in such cases because the psychopathology, or suffering of the soul, is so great that the ego, or rational dimension of the person, cannot contribute. No rational reason exists for why their child was killed instantly in an accident. It is impossible to feel better about a stillborn baby. No explanation comes to mind, and no comfort can be found in the news that your spouse is a sex addict. No doctor can explain away the terror of learning your loved one is dying of cancer. We all feel in the depths of our being the suffering that results from these tragedies. Healing and comfort are the only solace. But healing and comfort cannot come from a therapist, a priest, or a minister or from friends and loved ones. They are welcome companions on this journey, but healing comes from within—from the soul. Healing, in this sense, is not the same as a cure. Cancer patients can tell you they come to a sense of peace about their disease, even when they realize there is no cure. The healing comes when one is able to relinquish fear, anger, resentment, and terror to the regenerating energy of the soul. Some events cause us to grieve for a lifetime, but with inner healing we can live peacefully and return to a happy and fruitful life. What is necessary is to heal the wound and live with the scar.

Each person experiences the soul in their own personal way. Yet when we want to achieve intimacy or connect deeply with another person, we enhance that possibility by having conversations from the depths of our souls. When we allow for emotion in the form of tears or excitement, it is possible to get through almost any situation. We can learn to live with situations that are unfair, or do not make sense to us, or seem unresolvable. Living in peace with a chronic disease or gracefully accepting that your child will never mature beyond the mental age of a four-year-old is possible when you lay to rest your expectations of the future. Your choices and behavior will not be restricted by the fears and limitations of the ego. Rather, you will see possibilities and opportunities that you could not have otherwise imagined. I believe that life changes drastically when we can move below the surface of the ego, allowing life to be informed by the soul. We become someone we never imagined, living in compassion and empathy with others.

Intimacy is experienced only at the level of the soul. In fully accepting who you are, in playing your role in life's drama with all of your scars and abrasions and faults and failures, you present yourself to others and they accept you and love you. This is intimacy. This can happen during a sexual union, but it also happens when the addict comes to his loved one and admits he has slipped again and she says she is willing to go to Al-Anon and join his struggle. It comes when someone admits that she has overspent the budget by $25,000 and does not know how to pay it back—and her partner is willing to enter treatment with her. Intimacy comes with efforts to forgive and share the pathos of another. Intimacy comes when parents fall into one another's arms at the death of an infant. It comes when parents see their child graduate after their long financial struggle. Intimacy comes when we touch each other at a deep level.

This chapter completes Part I on behavior. Before we begin to look at communication, I recommend you take some time to reflect again on who you are and who you want to be. Take some time, minutes or even days, to reflect on the experiences of your life. What happened and why? Have you begun to accept all of it as a part of who you are? What you discover about yourself will be the basis for learning to communicate with integrity.

Points to remember about the soul:

- God is the mystery of creation, life, and death.
- The soul is not explained but experienced.
- The soul emanates from God and is the essence of life in each of us.
- The soul is not concerned with religion, monuments, or authority; rather, its concern is with wholeness and holiness, and with integration of body, mind, and spirit with God.
- The soul creates harmony and connects me with all of the universe and beyond.
- Awareness of the human soul must be a goal of each person's life journey and a personal opus, or great artistic work that requires a lifetime process of self-discovery.
- The soul is experienced by growing in wisdom and in virtuous interaction with other people and God through love, acceptance, non-judgment, forgiveness, and contemplation.
- Art, intimacy, nature, religion, relationship, and spiritual practice are the ways in which we experience the soul.
- The soul reveals itself to us through dreams and imagination, and this allows us to communicate with our conscious self.

- Dreams cannot be interpreted literally since they are not literal. Like parables, dreams convey a message through symbol, drama, and storytelling.
- One can give voice to the soul through spiritual disciplines such as prayer, meditation, contemplation, and other spiritual practice.
- Intimacy is experienced only at the level of the soul.
- What is felt from the soul cannot be explained adequately in words.
- The soul is not contained or directed by rules, moral codes, or laws, the things that are necessary for the ego to survive.

Part Two

HOW WE TALK ABOUT IT

Chapter 9

Communication Defined

Good communication is just as stimulating as black coffee, and just as hard to sleep after.

Anne Morrow Lindbergh, American writer

Types of communication

The word "communicate" is derived from the Latin *communicare*. It means *to impart, participate, and make known.* Another meaning is *to cause to pass from one to another,* as when a disease is communicated from one person to another. Still another interpretation suggests that something is transmitted and received. We can define communication, for our purposes here, as an act of giving and receiving—of imparting information and participating. Communication is a behavior. It is something that we do. To participate or not is a choice, a decision to be or not be involved. In Chapter 2 you learned something about your personality that will help you communicate with others or participate in a conversation. As you develop your personality and expand your experience, your communication skills will also expand. You will engage in dialogue with others in a more conscious and mindful manner.

To better understand the many ways we communicate in relationships, I think it is important to consider some definitions. Communication happens in many forms—and I have chosen to look at those that are most common. You will note that each is effective when used appropriately, but when misused, each becomes a form of miscommunication that can be annoying and destructive, often leading to heated arguments.

Interview

Have you ever tried to converse with a teen only to have this experience:

How was school today?

Fine.

What did you do?

Nothing.

How did your exam go?

Fine.

What else did you do at school?

Nothing. Why are you asking me all of these questions?

The same dynamic is seen in this exchange between a couple:

Hi, honey. What was your day like?

OK.

Anything new?

Nope.

In both examples one person is attempting to connect, the other is not really participating—he speaks but gives nothing, and they do not communicate. While this might be typical for a teenager, it is inappropriate non-communication for an adult. A better way would be this:

Hi, honey. What was your day like?

OK

Anything new?

Give me a little while to change, and I'll come in and tell you about it.

Good communication must be an exchange. Asking for time or telling the other you are not ready for conversation is good communication. Answering in monosyllables is not. When you say, *Yes, No, OK, Whatever* or emit various grunts and moans, you signify that you heard the other say something but you give nothing back. Sometimes, these words might really mean: *Leave me alone, Don't bother me,* or *I don't care about what you're saying.* Since the person speaking to you is attempting to engage in communication, your non-response implies: *I don't care about you.*

What has happened is that information has been sought, but the person asking (the interviewer) has received only a minimal answer to her question. Even though an exchange (or interview) has taken place, a real connection has not been made; close connection or intimacy has not been achieved.

Interview is a good form of communication, if you are looking for information. But it is not effective if your goal is to enter into a relationship.

Report

Often we expect information to be reported to us; we do not intend to give back. When we listen to the news, the radio, or a sporting event, we often talk back to the television or radio. But implicit is the understanding that our opinions or reactions will not be heard, will not be part of an exchange. However, in everyday relational exchange, this kind of communication is not acceptable. For instance, have you ever shared lunch with a friend who arrives just before the food is ordered? During the meal she talks continually, with no invitation for you to speak. Nor does she inquire about you in any way. When she is finished—with her food and her report—she stands and says: *This has been wonderful. We must do it again soon.* I cannot overemphasize how common this is. This same dynamic is often repeated in families when only the most dominant personalities speak up, while others never really get a chance to share what is on their mind.

Reporting as a method of communication can become a trap for couples who have lived together for many years. Because they know each other and their routines well, they often limit their interaction to a discussion of the day's agenda. The wife might relate to her husband what she did, who she saw, where she ate lunch, and what the traffic was like. While sharing this type of information is a good way for a couple stay in touch, it does not differ from the type of conversation either one of them might have with the check-out clerk at the grocery store. This type of exchange is not

Definitions of Psyche, Therapy, and Psychotherapy

The word "psyche" is an ancient Greek word meaning *soul, spirit,* or *mind.* Therapy comes from the Greek word "therapeia" and the Latin word "therapia," which both mean *curative* or *remedy.* Pschotherapy is understood as *healing the soul.*

an opening for intimacy, and it is important for couples to avoid sinking into a rut of communicating only at this level.

Lecture

Those of us who are teachers or instructors find this form of communication very tempting. However, most of us have learned that it can be a social turn-off. I remember my nineteen-year-old son saying to me: *Mom, I only asked you a question. I didn't ask you to teach me a class.*

Like most forms of communication, teaching has its place. Whether one is lecturing or preaching, it is important to know ahead of time if the listener is interested in what you will have to say. When you have information that you think might be valuable to impart to another, ask yourself: *Are you in a position to instruct this person? Is this information new and necessary to the listener? Is this information important?* If the answer to all of these is yes, then make it brief, personal, and meaningful.

A lecture can be demeaning to the listener. It is most evident in adult conversations with teenagers. When a teen receives instructions from a parent that he has heard over and over for years, he will not participate in the conversation. If the information has no real meaning to him, he will not listen. When the information seems impersonal, trivial, or irrelevant, it will not hold the teen's attention. This parent-teen dynamic is replicated in other environments where one person is presumed to have some level of influence over the other, such as husband to wife, wife to husband, or employer to employee. A typical response to a lecture is irritation.

Obsessive talk

The obsessive talker is the one who is intent on saying at all costs whatever is on her mind. She is the person who exhibits limited awareness of her listener. Often, she will stand too close without regard for her listener's personal space. She avoids or ignores social cues that signal the effect she is having on her listener. For instance, he moves away from her or indicates in some way that he wants to speak. He may look at something over her shoulder to let her know that he is has lost interest.

The obsessive talker leaves only enough space between her thoughts to take a breath. She might connect her sentences with the words "and" or "but" as she moves from one topic to another without stopping to listen. Others find her annoying and stress-inducing. The obsessive talker wreaks havoc in a meeting; every question pushes her "on" switch and it is impossible to turn her off. Those around her may recognize her impairment but are hesitant to approach her or ask for her opinion. When she is talking, the listener feels as if he is being held hostage, since a space does not exist in her monologue for him to make an exit. A listener can feel trapped when an obsessive talker is on the telephone, as well, especially if the listener cannot even get in a word to end the call.

Complaint

To take care of ourselves and see that our needs are met, we must know how to complain. It is not wrong to complain, but it can feel awful for both the speaker and the listener when it is done improperly. To complain is to express feelings of annoyance or dissatisfaction. We complain when we are suffering physical or emotional pain. As with all communication, it is important before speaking to reflect on what you will say and why. What is your intention? Is it important that you let someone know that you are dissatisfied, or do you just need to express that you are unhappy? If the problem is that you need a shoulder to cry on, whose shoulder will be offering you solace? If you are hoping for change, can you offer a constructive suggestion?

A genuine complaint should never be mistaken for whining. Whining is persistent complaining about your unhappiness, hoping that someone will come along to fix things and make you feel better. Whining is an immature way of getting attention and age appropriate to toddlers.

Argument

In an argument, one person tries to persuade the other to accept his view. It is not wrong or an example of miscommunication to argue a point. However, arguments become heated when the speaker is so set on his correct position that he cannot listen to another's opposite position. Also, communication breaks down when either party cannot support their bias with reason. Too often, the point of someone's argument is to imply that the other does not have a valid point of view.

During an argument, it is not unusual for tempers to rise and insults to fly. A valid argument is one in which each party states his bias and supports it with facts. Or he might say up front that he has no facts to support his view and is merely stating his opinion. Then he must allow equal time for the other to state her bias without interruption. In the end, both parties might continue to hold a different opinion.

Because arguments are ego-centered, they are based in fear. Remember that the ego part of our psyche is afraid of being diminished. When people feel challenged, it is natural for them to defend themselves. An immature reaction to being challenged can be defensive behavior that becomes aggressive. Yelling, name-calling, threats, and sarcasm are common defense mechanisms during arguments. Because they are not effective in resolving problems, people are tempted to bring up unresolved issues from the past. An argument can stir up resentments and hostility and impede intimacy. Family arguments can work best when the family dynamic allows time for everyone to make a point and no one feels threatened when others disagree.

Fighting

All couples fight, don't they? Well, actually, the answer is no, all couples do not fight. Nor should couples fight more often than any other two people. In fact, there is rarely a good reason for fighting. Yes, we do fight for our rights and fight disease, but, when referring to the dissension that happens between people, we use the definition that is closely aligned with attack, war, and injury. When couples, families, or siblings fight, the results are hurt feelings and an imbalance of power. One person feels powerless and fears that verbal or physical harm will come to him. He reacts to defend against perceived or real threat. He might use words to hurt the other in an attempt to cut him down to size. He attacks the other with verbal assaults like name-calling, insults, mocking, or mimicking, and may use foul language. The verbal bully uses the sound and pitch of his voice to intimidate or threaten the other. Fighting is competitive and divisive, creating a winner and a loser. One person must become the enemy and, eventually, the victim of the other.

Verbal bullying is a form of fighting that is never acceptable, but it is common in households, workplaces, and schools. Remember, the bully feels inadequate and instills fear in those around him to gain control and feel powerful. He uses his voice to threaten and intimidate others. Verbal bullying does not favor men; women are just as likely to threaten and manipulate with their voice and choice of words.

It is common in my therapy practice for a woman client to admit that she yells and screams at family members and loses respect for herself in the process. It is as if she believes the other will listen and understand better if she is shrieking. This always reminds me of one of my high school history instructors, a wonderful teacher with a German accent. Her students often raised their voices when speaking to her, apparently believing she would understand them better if they spoke loudly. *Please, I'm not deaf—I'm German,* she would explain.

Sometimes bullying behavior is passive-aggressive, and the aggressor attacks her victim with sarcastic criticism. Another way a passive-aggressive bully can assault someone is by completely ignoring his presence. I once attended meetings where the supervisor was threatened by the competence and professional attitude of one of the women in his department. He bullied her by ignoring her, pretending she was not in the room. He refused to look at her and ignored her comments, as if she had never spoken. His behavior had the desired effect—the woman found the meetings highly stressful and eventually became contemptuous of the supervisor. She struggled to keep his lack of communication from affecting her work. More important, this style of shunning is a common experience for those who are part of a minority. To pretend another is invisible is a primitive response to someone whose presence is threatening. It is meant to deny their existence as part of the group or family and is very hurtful and potentially psychologically damaging. It is also a silent form of bullying that communicates to the other that she has no value.

When parents are verbal bullies, they assault the budding self-esteem of their children. This type of parent uses fear and force to impose his will on someone who is vulnerable and unable to protect himself. A child should never have to cower before a parent. Yet, many parents yell and scream, intimidating their children, just as their parents behaved earlier toward them. This cycle can only be broken when one generation makes a conscious decision to choose their words and tone of voice more wisely.

Fighting and bullying are not acceptable methods of communication. Bullies violate their victim and leave long-lasting emotional scars. Like fighting, bullying is never appropriate in a relationship committed to love and growth.

Children learn how to speak and communicate from their parents or adult caregivers. Allowing fighting in the home can encourage sibling bullying. Several good studies are available online that show that sibling bullying has long-term effects. It certainly is a trend that I have observed in my years of work.

Talking in questions

Particularly annoying to me is the popular trend of ending every sentence by raising the pitch of one's voice, as in asking a question (I often find myself doing it). Some call this "uptalk." It is true that teens adopt ways of talking that are trendy and fun. But when adults are speaking, trendy talk is more distracting than engaging. I was told once that the definition of a speech impediment is a manner of speaking that calls attention to the way something is said rather than what is said. I don't think this is an adequate definition of a speech impediment, but it does work somewhat here.

Couching a question in sarcasm is demeaning and hurtful to the listener. This way of questioning, however, is more than annoying—it is abusive. For instance, couples and parents will often ask: *What did I tell you? What do I have to do to make you listen? What do I have to do to get through to you? Didn't we already talk about that?* As a rule, it is best not to ask a question when you already know the answer. It is more acceptable to restate the previously-made agreement or what you want the listener to hear: *I remember our conversation yesterday when we agreed that* . . . or *I explained this to you last week—I remember telling you* . . .

Meeting

The last thing working people want is to do is call a meeting. Yet pulling a group together to exchange views about a topic is an effective way to create a forum where everyone can speak their mind. In my opinion family meetings are essential. Sometimes the purpose is to make an announcement and hear everyone's response. Sometimes a discussion is necessary—like planning a vacation or scheduling an event. There are times when a family comes together to address a problem or a complaint or make an announcement.

I recently invited the family to gather so I could present our energy-use profile. I had obtained pie charts and graphs to accompany our monthly power statement to show how our family utilizes energy. It gave me an opportunity to show everyone how our efforts are paying off and to determine how our use compares with others in our area. This ten-minute gathering was informative and affirming to all of us.

I urge everyone to make a place in their lives for regular family or couple meetings and to use the time to define goals and expectations. I recommend to every couple that consults with me to set aside an hour or two on a weekend morning to reconnect and communicate. It is best to tackle difficult topics when both people are well rested and not pressed for time. My husband and I sit outdoors, sometimes on our front porch on Saturday or Sunday mornings, and enjoy tea and scones. During this time we recap the difficulties we faced and the fun we had during the previous week. It is a time when we are not hurried and are able to laugh and joke together. These "tea parties" have seen us through many difficult times and have provided a forum for us to review our shared lives and dream together. I recommend that couples teach their children to respect this special time and not interrupt them. Not only can children learn that their parents need time together alone, but couples are modeling respectful couple behavior. It is good for children to see their parents engaged in intimate, positive communication.

Writing and reading

When I have something important to communicate to family members, I like to write them a letter. If I want to share intimacy, provide guidance, or express concern, I find writing it down serves two purposes. First, the reader is paying attention and can reread parts of the letter to gain better understanding. Second, when the reader sets aside the letter to think about what I've written, she can always come back and look at it again. If the reader reacts negatively to the letter, she might understand it differently if she takes some time to reflect on its contents. Well-written letters that follow the guidelines for good communication can be very effective, and they may even one day be treasured by the receiver. Knowing this, I try to make my letters look appealing and neat, penning them on attractive stationery and using my best handwriting. I sometimes slip my notes into a greeting card that expresses my feelings about the reader.

Cyber talk

In my introduction, I made the point that verbal communication is diminishing in light of the many new ways people can utilize technology to "talk" with one another. I do get it. I have a Facebook page and several e-mail accounts, and texting has ended my habit of playing telephone tag with friends and clients. It is so much easier and convenient to respond "c u thurs" than to return a call or betray confidentiality by leaving a voice message. It is by far the most convenient way for a client to confirm or postpone an appointment or warn me they are stuck in traffic. My fear, though, is that we will lose the ability to talk with one another. It is much easier to sit at home and "techno-talk" with people, rather than meet with them or talk with them on the telephone.

Young people struggle with the skills they need to meet new people and to participate in a conversation. But opportunities to practice verbal interaction are limited when they do most of their communicating online or by texting. They need face-to-face communication skills to apply to college or for a job interview.

They must be able to speak well to participate in a college class, or to make an introduction, or even to express an opinion.

I don't want to pick on teens here because cyber communication can threaten adult relationships as well. Some couples tell me they text each other during the day but hardly speak in the evening. Others tell me they communicate mostly through e-mail. While this is quite convenient, it precludes eye contact, human touch, and hearing the sound of the other's voice. When it entirely replaces verbal communication, it is a barrier to intimacy. This is true with adults as well as with children. Children and teens need to hear their parents' voices. The sound of a loved one's voice, when used appropriately, touches the soul. A voice communicates intimacy, and teens and children, like adults, must experience intimacy in order to feel valued.

Touch used to emphasize words

The way you communicate will define the relationship you have with another person as casual, personal, collegial, or intimate. We use nonverbal cues to supplement speech. A roll of the eyes, a grimace, or body placement can either emphasize or nullify what it is that you are trying to say. We communicate nonverbally in a variety of ways. Whether utilizing a cold stare or a smile and a wink, words become clearer and more powerful with these nonverbal cues.

The use of touch is one of the most common things we do to supplement our words. Parents are often cautious about others touching their children, and children are taught to be cautious about allowing others to touch them. Yet children desperately need to be touched by trusted adults. People who live alone and do not share their life with a significant other might rarely feel the warm touch of another person. Older people often live away from family and friends and, though they talk together occasionally, they do not feel the physical warmth of another. Often they yearn for physical connection with others.

When I directed a women's center, I met many divorced and widowed women who yearned for the loving touch of a man. When my husband came to the center, as he often did, he greeted each woman with an embrace. The women often expressed how important this show of affection was to them. And, as you might guess, he enjoyed those hugs immensely as well.

The use of touch also defines our personal role in the relationship. We must always be mindful of personal boundaries when using nonverbal cues such as a handshake, an embrace, or touching another person. For instance, you might feel comfortable offering an embrace to a friend but not to your attorney. You might welcome a hug from your friends at church but not a kiss on the lips. You might be consoled by a touch on the arm from your therapist but feel uncomfortable with a hug.

To communicate through touch is natural and necessary. Humans need to be touched in a loving way. Yet we can never assume what is right for the other. Some people have only been hurt by the touch of others. Many children and teens are pushed, shoved, slapped, and hit. Many are sexually abused by the touch of another. Their association with touch is rooted in experiences that may have been hurtful. When these children become adults, they might prefer not to be touched at all. On the other hand, they may be starved for positive physical touch and intimacy and use touch in inappropriately intimate or sexual ways.

Touch is a social behavior that is learned and the value given to it is personal. Not everyone is comfortable with personal contact and a demonstration of feelings might confuse the other, who may feel embarrassed and imposed upon. We can never assume what will seem right to the other person.

When difficult opinions or critiques are expressed, they are more easily heard when accompanied with a loving touch. After a heated conversation, hurt feelings can be comforted with a hug or a touch on the back or the hand or even a handshake. Whether it is a three-year-old child completing a time-out or a teen who is restricted from driving the car, a hug and an *I love you* will communicate that the relationship has not been destroyed and the person is valued.

In a society where intimate touch has been tarnished by illicit and illegal behaviors that take advantage of others, we need to be continually mindful of the loving and healing power of communication through touch. I live by these rules: I hug each person in my family at least once a day, I never leave an ill or hurting person without hugging or touching her in a loving way, and I always seek permission to hug a stranger or a child, asking, *May I give you a hug?*or *May I take your little boy's hand?*

Apology is golden

I didn't do anything—why do I have to apologize? How many times have we heard children or teens utter this complaint? Yet often adults do no better. It is difficult and humbling to choose to apologize when we think the other's behavior caused the conflict. Until we understand the dynamic described in Chapter 5, we will find it difficult to apologize. To apologize is to accept responsibility for one's behavior. If you have done something hurtful or neglectful to another, take responsibility for your actions. If you have not misbehaved, recognize the feelings of the other. If the other feels hurt, it is because he thinks you did something hurtful. By now you understand that the other feels hurt because of her expectations of you. It is possible that you have behaved well and she still feels hurt. Recognize her hurt: *I'm sorry that you're sad* (or hurt, angry, disappointed). *I don't like to see you like this.* Add a positive and true statement: *Maybe we can talk about it again later* or *I know you had your heart set on the concert. I would love to see you go, but I just don't think it is safe* or *I know you're disappointed, but I just do not want to have company tonight—can we plan another time?* An apology can soothe hurt feelings without denying the integrity of your words or actions.

Whether you are part of a group, a marriage, a partnership, or any relationship with others, communication is the keystone of the relationship. When all parties can communicate well, most conflicts can be resolved effortlessly. Your level of communication will determine whether you live life on the surface or participate in an exchange at the deepest level, connecting with others in a soulful way.

Points to remember about communication:

- Good communication must be an exchange.
- Communication is verbal and nonverbal; both should be done well.
- An obsessive talker overpowers the listener. The listener feels trapped and concentrates instead on a getaway.
- Complaining is only appropriate when accompanied by a constructive suggestion.
- Whining can be defined as complaining because the person complaining is uncomfortable and looking for someone to rescue them. Whining is only appropriate for toddlers.

- Verbal assault is destructive and never appropriate in a relationship.
- When two people argue, each is taking a different view. Arguments are only effective in resolving problems when each person can substantiate their view with evidence. An argument can stir up resentments and hostility and impede intimacy.
- Fighting is never appropriate for couples or in family relationships. Fighting is competitive and divisive, typically resulting in a winner and a loser. One person must become the enemy and, eventually, the victim of the other.
- Bullying is a form of fighting and is very destructive to relationships. It can never be a part of a loving relationship.
- Talking in questions is annoying and distracting.
- Loving touch is important in communication. We cannot assume what type of touch is right for the other. It is important to respect personal boundaries.
- Inviting a group to exchange views about a topic is an effective way to create a forum where everyone can speak their mind. Family meetings and regular communication time for couples is essential for loving relationships.
- If you have done something hurtful or neglectful to another, take responsibility for your actions and apologize. If you have not misbehaved, recognize the feelings of the other.
- Good communication is the keystone of a loving relationship.

Chapter 10

The Art of Conversation

There is no conversation more boring than the one where everybody agrees.

Michel de Montaigne, sixteenth-century French writer

Personal expression

Three good reasons to engage in conversation are to exchange information, to get to know another person, and to seek companionship. Whether planned or spontaneous, good conversation follows a schema. Ideal communication allows people with different views of a topic to learn from one another. Each person's views originate in their perceptions. Good conversation respects that every participant has had different experiences and brings different viewpoints and feelings to the table. The table is a wonderful symbol for conversation for it is the setting for ingesting and digesting. Conversation is a time when we receive, or *ingest,* the words of another person and we *digest* those words, taking what we want to incorporate to expand our own views, or rejecting what does not seem useful to us. We set the scene for our time together. Families, friends, companies, and groups do best when conversation is a part of a daily routine.

Conversations take on the personality of the participants. This is obvious when a new person enters the conversation. The person presents new experiences, thoughts, and ideas. Everyone participating must integrate into the conversation, and the conversation should include all members of the group. Therefore the topics discussed should be of interest to everyone. Sometimes groups are formed with a special interest in mind such as finances, parenting, event planning, or business, when outsiders are not welcome. It is rude to have a conversation between two people that excludes others who are present or to discuss personal business in front of others who are not welcome to take part.

It is acceptable for some to be included only as observers. More introverted personalities prefer to observe and listen for a while before they enter the conversation. It is often more appropriate for teens and children to listen. The nineteenth-century ideal of *children should be seen but not heard* was still popular when I was a child. Of course we no longer believe this, but I wonder if we have not thrown out the baby with the bathwater. Some of my best childhood memories are of sitting with my mother and one of her friends, or the Avon lady, or the insurance man and listening to them talk. I learned how to talk with people by modeling my mother. I watched and listened as she laughed and teased and exchanged stories with her guests. I observed how she moved the tone of the conversation from lighthearted to serious. I heard her discuss local and national news, and I learned who she would vote for and why. I never thought about entering the conversation unless I was invited to do so.

I think it was during the 1970s and 1980s that the dynamic of children and conversation began to change. Children were encouraged to express themselves in an adult conversation. In some instances it even became acceptable for children to dominate the conversation. I certainly believe that children should be invited to participate in conversations. However, it is helpful to them and to the conversation if they are given some boundaries.

I remember one Sunday afternoon when a guest visited us and stayed for dinner. It is not uncommon in our family for everyone to talk at once with no one listening. Before dinner I asked our pre-teen and teenage granddaughters to follow some guidelines about table talk. I asked them to not speak unless they were sure they had something to say about the topic at hand. I encouraged them to think before they spoke and to make certain that whatever they were planning to say would be of interest to others, especially our guest. Our granddaughter, Juliann, opened the conversation (she opens most of our conversations) with: *I'm reading a good book, would anyone be interested in hearing about it?* Our guest responded, telling us that she was an avid reader and would love to hear about the book. Juliann revealed the title and author and gave a brief account of the story, and our guest was delighted.

We learned that our guest had a connection with children's books and was familiar with the series Juliann was reading. The conversation continued for several minutes and held everyone's interest. After dinner, Juliann expressed her satisfaction about having contributed to the conversation.

On another occasion my husband and I gave a holiday party. Although children were not on the guest list, we invited our granddaughters, who were then seven and eleven. We assigned them the duties of opening the door, greeting the visitors, and taking their coats. They were also instructed to clear away used dishes, silverware, and napkins but told to not speak unless they were directly spoken to. Many of our guests were delighted by their brief exchanges with them, and the girls were intrigued by the conversations they overheard. It was an important teaching moment for the girls, who felt respected and admired while they participated in an adult party.

Many good conversations accompany food and drink. When we invite our friends or family members to share a meal, it often leads to the telling of interesting stories and the forging of strong personal connections. Because of late work schedules and children's activities, dining together is becoming a thing of the past for many couples and families. Dinner conversation seems to be disappearing. Many people eat meals while watching television, which interferes with conversation. But shared meals invite shared conversation, and it would be a shame to see them go by the wayside. Although mealtime is ideal for conversation, it too often features bad manners and lack of self-control. It is not unusual to observe a family in a restaurant with young children who are talking loudly, teens who are texting, and silent parents who are ignoring everyone. What has happened to conversation—the exchange of experiences, feelings, and opinions? Has mealtime become a time to dine and dash instead of a time for connecting at a personal level while sharing food?

Alcohol, in moderation, can accentuate a good conversation. A glass of wine or mug of cold beer can foster a mood of relaxation and acceptance. On the other hand, alcohol can also be a detriment to conversation. People tend to get irritated and defensive when they are under the influence of alcohol, and they are less accepting of the behavior of others. When alcoholic beverages are served, it is essential that the conversation not turn to controversial or sensitive topics. People are more apt to react than to respond.

Casual conversations are spontaneous. Important conversations, with a designated outcome and intention, are better when they are planned. Because important conversations cannot be rushed and require full attention, they are best held before 8 p.m. At a later time in the evening participants are often too tired to think rationally and too impatient to respond well. Late-night conversation might turn into an argument that becomes violent. Fatigue, alcohol, and drugs mixed in with a discussion of sex, finances, and personal responsibilities and expectations make a toxic cocktail that often precedes domestic violence.

Rules of etiquette exist (often unspoken) that apply to conversation, and they guide the discourse. Since conversation is an exchange of ideas and experiences between or among people, time must be found for each person to express themselves. While speaking, it is important to use a tone that is inviting and interesting. A good speaker will limit the amount of time he spends talking and avoid repeating himself. His tone of voice, eye contact, and pleasant manner will invite rather than challenge a response from those he is speaking to.

Those who are receiving, or listening, must assume a posture of openness. They must respect what the speaker is saying, accepting that he is giving his own opinion. Listeners accept that his thoughts and opinions may differ from their own. If the speaker chooses his words poorly or says something in an unusual way, it is not the listener's responsibility to change the speaker's words or correct his thoughts. The speaker's manner, opinions, and beliefs are received as his truth, and he is allowed enough time to express himself fully and without interruption. If he talks obsessively and does not allow for others to respond, a listener must signal that it is her turn. If she is confused or if she thinks his words do not make sense, she can ask for clarification: *I'm not clear about what you're saying; can you explain again?* or *I have a different view. Can I tell you how I see it?* It would be inappropriate, however, to say: *What you're saying is wrong* or *That doesn't make sense.*

If the speaker holds to his truth and is not interested in hearing the listener's views, the conversation is over. It is best to change the topic to one that is less intense or controversial and more acceptable to both parties. To try and argue a point with someone who is unwilling to expand his views or listen to the other's views is futile and often ends with hurt feelings and a damaged relationship. An effective conversation must be open-ended, allowing each person to express themselves to the best of their ability.

When I take this stance in personal interactions with family, friends, and co-workers, I find that my perception of life and acceptance of others becomes richer and more welcoming. Openness enhances a relationship and expands perception:

I'm interested in why you think curfew should be midnight.

I'm not sure we should have another child. Will you listen to my concerns?

I have never been to the Southwest. What do people in your area think of our current immigration law?

I have never spoken with a Muslim. Can you tell me something about your beliefs? Do you mind if I ask questions?

I cannot understand why you voted for John Doe; what do you think he brings to the table?

A good and energetic conversation is formed around differing opinions that are expressed well. Groups that include people who seem to have little in common can lead to the most interesting conversations. Neighbors in a diverse community can have wonderful exchanges. When people of the same religion, the same culture, and the same family configuration come together, they may have little to say after catching up on personal events. Sometimes people feel pressured to attend a company party or a family dinner. They go because they fear the repercussions if they do not attend, although they are anticipating the same conversations that have happened many times before: *How are you? How are the kids? Johnny is going to school now, right? How's work going? Do any golfing lately?* and so on. Members of an extended family or coworkers from an office often have a polite exchange with others and then leave. What inhibits a group like this from engaging in a stimulating conversation? It is probably a fear of being judged or a fear of someone being hurt or angry.

Some groups are able to behave politely when they come together for no other reason than to meet one another. A cocktail party before a business meeting is a good example of people getting together to meet one another, but not necessarily to begin a relationship or make a personal connection.

Family groups sometimes limit themselves to a similar connection. Arguably, we live in more diverse communities than ever before, yet many people carefully avoid controversy and discuss only what they have in common, avoiding their differences. Many still shy away from the big three dangerous topics: sex, politics, and religion. Yet it is in sharing our differences that we invite good conversation and close relationships. Family members are hesitant to say anything that might lead to dissension or criticism; it is as if there is an unspoken rule that goes something like this:

> *We all like each other here. We don't want any arguing or anybody's feelings to be hurt. We must only talk about what we agree on, and if we do not agree, we must keep our thoughts and opinions to ourselves; we must play it safe. If someone gets out of line, raising his voice or expressing hurt feelings, we must make sure to help that person feel better. We must comfort and console and avoid anything that will cause disagreement or conflict. To confront an idea or belief would make us disagreeable, and we certainly don't want to be disagreeable.*

In this environment, caution is the key word: *Be careful not to reveal any part of you that would seem disagreeable to another.* Because each member of the group believes they are responsible when another feels embarrassed, hurt, confused, or disappointed, everyone remains nice and polite and careful. The problem that arises, though, is that the gathering can become superficial and opportunities for intimacy are jeopardized.

Keeping communication at this level sends a message that the group wants to avoid any kind of conflict, making it difficult for someone to talk about their financial or marital difficulties.

And it is not a safe place for a young person to come out and tell his family that he is gay. It also prevents those who are being sexually abused or harassed by someone in the group to speak up. If one family member is struggling with a mental or emotional illness, they will not feel accepted if they disclose it. If a family member is living in an abusive relationship, he will cover his scars, emotional and physical, rather than allow others to know about it.

A family that is not open to the messy details of their lives sets a tone that says to members they must first and foremost *present as nice people who follow the rules.* When a member is not feeling nice, she will not risk revealing her true self and may just stay away. This attitude is frequently encountered by those who work with the emotionally ill. Often a person will take antidepressants or similar medications that affect the central nervous system. Yet they do not want family, even spouses or friends, to know they are suffering from depression, anxiety, and mood swings. They do not want anyone to find out they are living in deep pain. It is not uncommon for a family member to commit suicide before others are aware that she has been suffering from severe depression. Often it is only when someone announces that they are getting a divorce that others close to them realize the marriage was in distress.

While people often enter or begin conversations to exchange ideas, I think the vast majority of conversations are about enhancing companionship. People want to connect. Everyone has a story to tell that is unique to them. People dress up their stories with humor and embellish them to entertain their listeners. We like to laugh at ourselves and at the antics of others. If a person does not feel good about himself, he is less likely to laugh at himself. But when a person does tell a story about himself or relates an anecdote, and it is accepted well by others, his self-esteem increases. When children or teens tell stories about themselves, and are accepted by others, they begin to feel part of the group and recognize that what they have to offer is valuable.

Strong family groups provide a venue for children to sing, dance, recite, and play musical instruments. Children gain confidence when they can depend on their family members to affirm and appreciate them. They know they will not fail when they perform before their supportive family members. Family affirmation is like having training wheels on the road to strong self-esteem.

Conversation is an art that can be expected to improve with practice. Good conversation increases vocabulary and heightens perceptions of life. Conversation connects us with others through an exchange of ideas, stories, and laughter.

Points to remember about good speakers and listeners:

A good speaker:

- Monitors tone of voice.
- Speaks respectfully to others.
- Invites a response from others.
- Allows time for a full response without interrupting.
- Chooses words wisely and does not use sarcasm.
- Is able to laugh at himself.
- Paces himself, taking care to express himself well.
- Will be responsible for his statements.
- Is a good listener.
- Does not monopolize the conversation.

A good listener:

- Does not argue with the speaker.
- Does not finish the speaker's sentences.

- Is attentive, focusing on the speaker's words, meanings, and pauses.
- Allows the speaker enough time to express herself fully and without interruption.
- Is eager to consider the speaker's point of view.
- Comes to the table with an open mind.
- Realizes her perceptions are limited to her experiences and that she can learn from others.
- Respects feelings and emotions as an intimate expression of the other.

Chapter 11

Developing a Personal Style

Self-expression must pass into communication for its fulfillment.

Pearl S. Buck, American writer

Your words speak for you

Whether you want to develop good communication skills from scratch or improve the ones you already have, this chapter will give you an overview of what works for most people. To learn to communicate well, you must incorporate everything you know about yourself. For instance, if you have a personality that leans to introversion, you will be more comfortable listening. You will prefer a slower pace in conversation with time to think about your responses. You might struggle with understanding how to begin and end a conversation.

If your personality leans more to extroversion, you will be more comfortable talking. Waiting for the other to respond might be a challenge for you. You might find yourself speaking for the other and finishing her sentences, and you might be uncomfortable with silences. I recommend that you observe yourself in conversation to see if you can identify your weak spots. The skills you will need might not come naturally to you, but you can learn them.

It's all about you

In Chapter 5 you learned that, in most instances, your behavior is a result of your personal choices and decisions. Nobody other than you is responsible for your behavior. This rule also applies to communication. The only view you can genuinely express is your own. Whether you are referring to a topic, person, feeling, event, or behavior, you can only talk about your experience of it. You cannot accurately say what another thinks or feels; you can only share your interpretation and response to what he tells you. You cannot accurately determine what another wants or needs but can only determine what you anticipate another wants or needs. Many communication breakdowns are caused when one person makes incorrect assumptions about another.

You will ultimately be the type of communicator that you choose to be. You may be aggressive and mean-spirited or kind and respectful. Some people choose to be quiet and withdrawn, while others are brash and overbearing. Some people choose their words and articulate their views well. Others might develop the habit of peppering their conversation with foul words, communicating to others their poor self-esteem and meager vocabulary. Some will depend on useless words like "whatever" to keep them safe from expressing themselves at all. You, however, will be different. Since there is no one like you, your communication will be unique—reflecting you.

To communicate in a genuine way, you can only express what *you* have experienced and what *you* think and feel, and only *you* can explain your behavior. Again, this does not mean that you are the most important focus and that others should be interested only in you. Rather it means that you are all you know. You are responsible for your behavior or how the opinions, feelings, and behavior of others affect you. Therefore, your communication will be in the first person: *I want* or *I need* or *I think you mean.* Nobody can argue with what you think or feel. Others can disagree with you, though, and say they think something different. But that difference does not invalidate your view, and both opinions can stand as truth. For example, Polly and Alice are discussing the behavior of a mutual friend:

> Polly: *She makes me so angry. She thinks everybody should do it her way. I'm tired of her moods and pouting. She is not coming here again.*
>
> Alice: *I hear what you're saying. I see it differently. I don't know what she thinks, but I don't pay attention to her pouting. That's just her. I just do what I want and don't let her mood affect me. I like to be with her most of the time.*

Polly struggles more with their friend because she believes the friend is responsible for her (Polly's) anger. She tries to read her friend's mind to understand what she is thinking. She believes she is responsible somehow for their friend's moods and adapts her behavior to her moods, instead of being herself. Having a friendship like this is exhausting. But Alice speaks in "I" statements. She realizes that she is responsible for how she feels and what she does, and this is reflected in the way she forms her responses. Polly could express herself in another, more empowering, way:

> *I get so upset when I'm with her. I am affected by her moods, and I don't know what she is thinking. I don't understand why she gets so negative, and I need to have a talk with her soon to better understand her.*

Now Polly is talking about herself. She has the power to change the situation and get to know her friend better. In my experience, friends like this can be manipulative and an attempt to understand them can be difficult. You must address your words to the person she is when she is not in a mood. Remember, she is not her mood and she may not know why she is in the mood, or that she is in a mood at all. Always remember when you communicate that you are only expressing yourself and not anyone else. To begin a comment with *You* or *She* or *They* is to begin with a judgment or an accusation. This can feel like a verbal attack to the other and invites a defensive and sometimes counterattacking response. Arguments are often comprised of subtle attacks and counterattacks. Let's look at Polly's conversation with her friend:

> *We need to talk. Your moods get on my nerves. You get me so down when we're together because you are always so negative. What is your problem? I don't know if you can be my friend. I've already talked with Alice about you, and she feels like me.*

This approach, which is very common, is sprinkled with judgments, accusations, and subtle attacks. Polly even finishes her barrage by letting her friend know that she has already gossiped about her to their mutual friend. Her friend, I would guess, feels hurt or angry, and this will probably start a hurtful exchange. Polly's aggressive attitude has put her in a one-up position and drawn Alice into the situation. A better way to speak to her friend would have been like this:

> *I have some concerns about our friendship. The last few times we have been together I have left feeling irritated. It seems to me that you get upset when we don't do things your way. I'm not sure if you are unhappy with me or if there is something wrong in our friendship. I wasn't sure how to tell you this because I don't want you to be hurt. I did talk with Alice first because I am not sure how to approach you without saying something hurtful.*

This better way allows the friend to know what Polly is experiencing and feeling. Polly does not really know what her friend thinks or if she has a problem. If said with kindness, this opening from Polly invites a deeper sharing from her friend. It allows her friend to give an explanation rather than a defense. Polly sets up an environment that can allow her friend to say something like this:

> *I don't know why I get in these moods, and I am troubled by them too. I do it around my family and other friends. I don't know why I feel so depressed and negative sometimes.*

But this exchange presumes that the friend has good communication skills. Suppose she does not, which is often the case. She might respond like this:

> *What are you talking about? You act like I'm always in a bad mood. What about your moods? You're not so perfect!*

Just because Polly utilizes the correct skills and makes an attempt to be assertive does not mean that her friend will respond in the same way. This possible response, like the first Polly example, is filled with counterattacks that turn the conversation around to make Polly the object of derision. If Polly feels attacked, it will take self-restraint not to respond defensively, which could happen even if the speaker did not attack. It is difficult for many to hear feedback about their behavior if their experience informs them that feedback is an attack or criticism. When this dynamic occurs, the conversation is out of control. Polly will do best, and stay in control of herself, if she responds in this way:

> *I was actually talking about myself. I'm just trying to understand you better. Maybe we can talk about it another time. I treasure your friendship and hope we can continue as friends.*

This response will end the exchange on a positive note. Polly's friend has something to think about, and she may or may not examine her behavior and make a change. If not, Polly will most likely put some emotional distance between them, in order to maintain the friendship. A good conversation can clear the air and strengthen the relationship. But the chance is real that a dysfunctional relationship will end.

As you learned above, conversation is about speaking and listening. It amazes me how many adults in a family relationship or couple relationship never talk. Some couples are married for years and do not know each other as well as I know them after two sessions. They assume they know what the other wants and needs. They might live in what seems like a peaceful environment but is actually a dead environment. There is never a conflict or disagreement, but neither is there a spark of life. Too often a parent is emotionally separated from the family or one spouse is not emotionally available to the other. Instead, they agree on a flat-line kind of existence, avoiding any chance of conflict. Yet conflict, when resolved, gives new life to a relationship. It clears the air between people and makes room for new ideas and activities.

Your style of conversing with others is something that develops. Like all your talents, with your first efforts you might feel nervous and incompetent. It takes time and practice to master your conversation skills. First you must show up, or enter into dialogue with another—you must say something. Second, you must practice your skills—you might imitate a style you have heard and expand your vocabulary. Try using new words until you are comfortable with them. And trust yourself—you will make mistakes and perhaps even put your foot in your mouth more than once. But mistakes can be corrected, and you will find an appropriate way to take back what you've said. Use your voice as an instrument, being aware of tone, tempo, and volume. And remember that your words reflect who you are. They are the way you introduce yourself to the world.

Points to remember about how to communicate well:

- Your personality type influences the way you participate in conversation.
- Your words represent you.
- The only view you can genuinely express is your own. Whether you are referring to a topic, person, feeling, event, or behavior, you can only talk about your experience of it.
- Communication breakdowns are caused when one person makes incorrect assumptions about another.
- To begin a comment with *You* or *She* or *They* is to begin with a judgment or an accusation. This can feel like a verbal attack to others.
- Just because you use correct skills and make an attempt to be assertive does not mean that your listener will respond in the same way. When this happens, be ready to explain that you are expressing yourself, not judging your listener.
- Conversation is about speaking and listening; it is an exchange of views and experiences.
- Conversation is an art that must be learned and practiced until it is the best verbal expression of you.

Chapter 12

Living Large

Appreciation is a wonderful thing: it makes what is excellent in others belong to us as well.

Voltaire, French philosopher

Going public

In the eleven previous chapters, I have focused on personal and interpersonal behavior and communication. I have emphasized that a lack of knowledge or self-awareness interferes with our ability to understand and change behavior and that a lack of personal skills and vocabulary limits our ability to communicate well with others.

It may have occurred to you that these personal skills can also be applied on a larger scale to more universal or collective behavior and communication, involving much larger groups like communities and countries.

Public conversation, like personal or private conversation, is best when it begins with reflection and a commitment to basic truth. It is best when the speaker and listener have the ability to move the conversation to a soul level. At this level there is no room for deceit, meanness, or attacks and no need to make the other accept a particular belief or practice. Responsible behavior and communication result in self-respect and the ability to respect the dignity of others, however different they may be.

Sociopathy and leadership

A refusal to listen to and care about others at a soul-conscious level has resulted in horrific arguments and wars since the beginning of time. Just as a married couple can battle for years without coming to a peaceful acceptance, geographical neighbors and religious sects continue to battle and initiate wars because they will not listen to the other and concede that the other's truth might have some merit. All humans, it seems, do not have the ability to acknowledge that another group's truth is different than ours, or that their god is a reflection of their experience and is as authentic to them as ours is to us. We camouflage our desire to take others' resources and enslave them by asserting fraudulent moral purpose. Or we shun them and deny them their rights and safety, employing moral platitudes to defend our mean, oppressive, and sociopathic behavior.

Mincing words

The battles that are fought when religious traditions or doctrines are threatened are called holy wars and receive the blessings of religious authorities; when war is generated by countries, the behavior is considered patriotic. Many people go against their basic personal values because they are too afraid or confused to buck those in power. It is as if the world, too, has an ego that lives in fear of threat or death and must fight to the end anything that challenges it or threatens its safety or comfort.

Those in power use this national fear to their benefit and construct large followings of people who cannot recognize that the underlying motives of their leaders are power and greed and a need to control others. When we can identify sociopaths in our families, our workplaces, and our communities, we can learn to recognize sociopaths who run for political office. They play out their behavior on a much grander scale, and it can take decades to rectify their immoral acts. We will make better choices when we learn that every group, nation, corporation, and community includes sociopaths in leadership positions, because that is where sociopaths can be found. Sociopaths gravitate to places where power is available to them. Their path to the top is colored with deceit, self-interest, and manipulation, and they almost always have a smooth-talking and winning personality.

When we observe current events or anticipate the future, it may be difficult to identify sociopaths, because they are much easier to spot after the fact, when we can observe the ruined lives, devastation, and death they leave in their wake. For example, if investors had recognized the Ponzi scheme of Bernie Madoff, they would not have participated. But who knew? Friends, relatives, and strangers were won over by Madoff's friendly manner and self-confidence. The man was very convincing. Yet one must question whether there was ever an intention on his part to make legal investments that would benefit his victims. His actions were calculated, manipulative, and devious.

Diversity

When we can accept the diversity in our own community and workplace, we will be able to accept the importance of diversity on a global scale. When we can drop the persona of superiority or righteousness and listen to those who appear to be different from us, we will be able to appreciate the extraordinary richness of the cultures and beliefs of other people. Perhaps when we realize that soulful people are found in every country and culture, we will have the confidence and integrity to begin a conversation with them.

If we learn to communicate effectively among the diverse groups in our own communities, we may be able to learn to communicate better on a global scale. Our global community has not learned to interact peacefully. We spend billions of dollars to ready ourselves to defend what we consider to be ours, but we are not equipped to live peacefully side by side. It seems that the focus of malfeasance is to become all-powerful and capture the wealth of the world rather than to live peacefully with one another.

Most of us have listened to a disagreement taking place between two people who are unable to understand that their argument is ridiculous because neither of them is making sense; frequently they are using different (and often meaningless) words to argue the same point. To engage in an intelligent national conversation, we, or our representatives, must employ the same skills required to have an intelligent personal conversation. A national discussion must be grounded in truth and supported by facts. Listeners, or political constituents, are wise to know the facts before their representatives speak for them. The same rules apply to an intelligent personal conversation.

Secular vs. religious values

Our limited vocabulary hinders our ability to have an intelligent conversation on a national level, just as it does in our private lives on a personal level. I find it disturbing that there is so much fear that the United States is becoming a secular rather than a religious nation. Too often I hear the word "secular" discussed in a way that supposes that something secular has no moral value. Nothing could be further from the truth. Secular more often describes the basic values of a group. Secular does not describe values that are anti-religious; rather, it includes the basic human values of all religions and cultures.

The phrase "family values" is often mistaken to mean the morality of fundamental Christian religious views, as if the values of Jewish, Muslim, or Hindu families are vastly different. But family values are not much different than the basic human values that are rooted in the need for survival. Most people want their families to have enough food and clean water and air to maintain good health. They want for them adequate housing and health care and protection from emotional and physical abuse. Most people want the right to protect their families and to acquire the necessities that allow their families to thrive. All of us want the right to practice our cultural and religious traditions without fear. Even though a secular belief does not require that we attend a worship service regularly, it does protect our right to do so. A true secular value is not in conflict with religion unless a particular tradition of one group undermines the rights of others in the group.

To understand secular values, we must understand that they are the umbrella that incorporates the basic values of each of the particular groups within the whole, while not favoring one particular group over another. In a family, for example, we can see that it is good practice to establish an 8 p.m. bedtime for a toddler, yet other family members prefer a 10 p.m., 11 p.m., or later bedtime. The underlying value is that each family member get the proper amount of sleep, not that all members are in bed early; all family members are not required to follow the same rule. If a teen prefers to stay awake until 1 a.m., the leaders of the family will probably decide that this choice opposes the basic family value and will block his personal choice.

In a communal setting, we see this same type of conflict repeating every year when people quarrel about celebrating Christmas rather than "the holidays." Yet the word "holiday" is a derivative of the words "holy days." Most cultures have holy days and wish to celebrate them. Many will agree that their holy days can be celebrated during autumn, winter, and early spring. Still, many feel slighted because their particular holy day does not claim the season; instead they think the word holiday is a denial rather than an acceptance of their particular belief. Listening to and learning from others will avoid this conflict and allow the larger group to honor their diverse traditions.

Afterword

This is a book about behavior and communication, but also about so much more. I have attempted to give the reader the best of what is addressed in a typical therapy session, when healing the soul is the goal. Too often people avoid getting the help they need in resolving conflicts, treating an emotional illness, or healing relationships because they fear they will be told that something is wrong with them. Discerning what is wrong with someone is not a therapeutic goal. The goal is to discover the goodness in someone, to discover her potential to be wonderful, and to help her to find her place of peace and harmony in the world. Psychotherapy should be fun. Learning about yourself and identifying stumbling blocks along the way is incredibly freeing. Yes, a lot of tears may be shed along the way. But tears are like taking a shower from the inside out. We feel so much better after a good cry and are able to think so much more clearly. Tears are nature's best way of relieving anxiety and stress. I remember a client who once told me: *I can't believe I look forward to coming here every week to cry—and I pay you for it! What's wrong with this picture?*

Over a lifetime we often feel unsettled about our lives, whether due to a major life change or just plain boredom. At such times we feel unsatisfied or empty or discouraged. These feelings alert us to our need to change—to turn the page or begin a new chapter in our lives. Sometimes the urge will prompt us to begin a new book of our life—we might be called to move to another country or begin a new career. The American mythologist Joseph Campbell encouraged us to "follow our bliss." When we respond to these deep longings, it requires us to have a good sense of ourselves. Rather than concentrating on endings, we are always beginning. Perhaps this book will accompany a new beginning for you.

My hope is that this book will guide the reader to enter into responsible conversation and to communicate well. The ability to do this is based on self-awareness and an understanding of the needs and experiences of the other. I hope the reader will be open to entering into public conversations, whether with a school board, a city council, a state legislature, or the U.S. Congress.

Acknowledgments

My deepest thanks for help with writing this book go to the many clients who have trusted me with their stories and secrets for so many years. It is customary to caution budding therapists against forming personal and social relationships with clients. I believe I have handled this pretty well, but in one area I admit complete failure: I have fallen in love with them all. I can remember almost all of their names and with a hint or two I can even remember their stories. We have laughed and cried together, and our sessions have been memorable and fun. My clients have played an important role in the person I have become and taught me many things.

I began my therapist career as a rather shy listener, fearing I would not know what to say or how to tend to clients in their sadness or pain. They have shaped me into a confident and wise woman. I have been privileged to share in the lives of mothers, fathers, pregnant teens, those recovering from addictions, and so many who have risen like phoenixes from the ashes of devastated lives. I have witnessed courage, dedication, and tenderness beyond belief as my clients have struggled to save marriages, repair friendships, confront life-threatening illnesses, and stand by adult children with emotional illnesses or brain disorders. I am blessed to have been the one to welcome them as they bared their souls while feeling hopeless and asking for a reason to live. I could never have become the person I am without them and the trust they have turned over to me. Many have asked for this book and even more have hoped that their stories might become a source of hope for others.

I extend my gratitude to William J. Bulay, M.Div. and Diplomate Jungian Analyst, who introduced me to the work of

Carl Jung and generously guided my early work. Bill mentored me in bringing Jung's personality theory and dream work alive in marriage and family therapy.

I gratefully acknowledge the community of St. Thomas a'Becket Catholic Church in Canton, Michigan, for their consistent encouragement of me in the writing of this book. My contributions to the weekly paper *The Chancellor* were opportunities for me to challenge myself. Ten years of their feedback, both positive and negative, helped me to find my writing "voice."

When I began the actual writing process, I found it difficult because I have always considered myself a presenter and not a writer. When I teach, I am spontaneous—laughter and fun are at the heart of my presentations. Writing for me was entering into a new world that involved talking to an audience I could not see. I had some words on paper, a workable outline, and a sense of direction when I met Robert H. Miller. Rob was a giant step ahead of me, then in the process of publishing his first book, *Hidden Hell: Discovering My Father's POW Diary.* Rob's amazing excitement for his work, and mine, became contagious. He was generous with his support and suggestions and became my strong advocate. On days when I had scheduled time to write, but couldn't seem to get going, I only needed to call on Rob. He travels a lot for his work, and wherever he was in the world, I would hear from him. He knew just what to say to get the wheels turning again and push me through my writer's block.

Rob generously introduced me to Penny Schreiber, his gifted editor. Penny became my editor and helped me to become a writer. She reined me in when I went off on a tangent. Her notes within the text (for example: *I have no idea what this means or how this fits in*) took me to task. She brought out my best words and has given me hope that I will continue to learn and become an excellent writer. Penny has been a great midwife to me as I gave birth to this work.

I extend my gratitude to Nancy Rabitoy, who so artfully designed the interior and cover of this book. She allowed me to play with ideas and respected my need to follow my intuition and find my way. Nancy got to the heart of this book with a design that it deserves.

I also must thank my "sister" and friend Debbie Miller, who feeds my soul. Our weekly lunches helped me to stay with the project when there were so many distractions. Our laughter and foolishness remind me that everything can be fun. Debbie's words "Keep with it, Patty, you're a good writer" helped me to continue to believe in myself and see purpose in my work.

I am thankful to my fellow therapist Marty Kurylowicz for his time and conversation regarding the soul as the heart of our work. Marty was very generous in reviewing my vignettes and giving me professional feedback and encouragement. I am fortunate to share this profession with him.

Another "sister" and friend, Fran Culverhouse, has been a favored and constant companion in the journey of my work. I say thank you to her for years of conversation on a shared spiritual journey and for her assistance in writing about the soul.

Most of all I want to thank my husband, John Danks, my best friend and companion in my life's journey. We have faced life head-on. He has supported me in sharing examples of our life together to illustrate lessons that have helped us grow as individuals and as a couple. Although we have tumbled over a few cliffs together, he has always been more than willing to dust us off and start again. John's courage has sustained me in the life situations that enrich this work. He has kept our home and family intact, generously waiting on me and giving me time to write or be alone and quiet so that ideas could germinate and find expression. I am so grateful.

Sources

Below are the sources I have consulted for this book:

Chapter 1: Understanding Behavior

Cannon, W. B. (1929). *Bodily changes in pain, hunger, fear, and rage: An account of recent research into the function of emotional excitement.* 2nd Ed. New York: AppletonCenturyCrofts.

Churchland, Patricia S. (2011). *Braintrust.* Princeton: Princeton University Press.

Kral, V. A. & MacLean, Paul D. (1973). *A Triune concept of the brain and behavior.* Toronto: Univ. of Toronto.

MacLean, Paul D. (1990). *The triune brain in evolution: Role in paleocerebral functions.* New York: Plenum Press.

Chapter 3: When Others Cannot Change

American Psychiatric Association. (1994). *Diagnostic and statistical manual of mental disorders.* 4th Ed. American Psychiatric Publishing, Inc.

Bancroft, Lundy. (2003). *Why does he do that? Inside the minds of angry and controlling men.* New York: Berkley Books, Penguin Group, Inc.

Hare, Robert D. (1993). *Without conscience: The disturbing world of the psychopaths among us.* New York: The Guilford Press.

Kessler, R. C. et al. (2005). *Prevalence, severity, and comorbidity of twelve-month DSM-IV disorders in the National Comorbidity Survey Replication. Archives of General Psychiatry,* Jun; 62(6): 617-27.

Kiehl, Kent A. & Buckholtz, Joshua W. *Inside the mind of a psychopath.* Scientific American Mind. September/October, 2010.

Kiehl, Kent A. et al. (2001). *Limbic abnormalities in affective processing by criminal psychopaths as revealed by functional magnetic resonance imaging.* Biological Psychiatry, 2001; 50: 677–684.

Robins, L. N. & Regier, D. A., eds. (1991). *Psychiatric disorders in America: The Epidemiologic Catchment Area Study.* New York: The Free Press.

Seabrook, John. (2008). *Suffering souls: The search for the roots of psychopathy.* New York: The New Yorker.

Stout, Martha. (2005). *The sociopath next door.* New York: Broadway Books.

Chapter 4: Know Yourself

Baron, Renee. (1998). *What type am I? Discover who you really are.* New York: Penguin Books.

Jung, Carl Gustav (1971). *Psychological types.* Coll. Works of C. G. Jung, Vol. 6. Princeton, NJ: Princeton University Press.

Keirsey, David & Bates, Marilyn. (1978). *Please understand me: Character and temperament types.* Hong Kong. Distributed by Prometheus Nemesis Book Company, Del Mar, CA.

Myers, Isabel Briggs. (1980). *Gifts differing: Understanding personality type.* DaviesBlack Publishing; Reprint edition (May 1, 1995). ISBN 089106074X

Pearman, R. & Albritton, S. (1996). *I'm not crazy, I'm just not you: The real meaning of the sixteen personality types.* Mountain View, CA: DaviesBlack Publishing.

Storr, Anthony (Editor). (1999). The essential Jung: Selected writings. Princeton, NJ: Princeton University Press.

Chapter 5: It's All About You

Al-Anon Family Group Headquarters, Inc. Staff. (1992). Courage to change one day at a time in Al-Anon II. Virginia Beach: Al-Anon Family Group Headquarters, Inc.

Bandura, A. (1973). Aggression: A social learning analysis.Englewood Cliffs, NJ: Prentice-Hall.

Chapter 6: Developing a Personal Behavior Style

Baldrige, Letitia. (2003). New manners for new times: A complete guide to etiquette. New York: Scribner.

Crisp, Quentin. (1985). Manners from heaven: A divine guide to good behavior. New York: Harper Collins Publishers.

Farley, Thomas P. (2005). Town & Country modern manners: The thinking person's guide to social graces. New York: Hearst Books.

Martin, Judith. (2005). Miss Manners' guide to excruciatingly correct behavior. New York: W. W. Norton & Company.

Post, Peggy. (2004). Emily Post's etiquette. 17th Indexed Edition. New York: Harper Resource.

Vaillant, George E. (1992). Ego mechanisms of defense: A guide for clinicians and researchers. Washington, DC: American Psychiatric Press.

Chapter 7: Assertive Behavior

Alberti, Robert E. & Emmons, Michael L. (2008). *Your perfect right: Assertiveness and equality in your life and relationships,* 9th Ed. California: Impact Publishers.

Austin, Nancy (1987). *The Assertive woman: A new look.* San Luis Obispo, CA: Impact Publishers.

Chapter 8: Deepening Awareness

Hillman, James. (1997). *The Soul's code: In search of character and calling.* New York: Grand Central Publishing.

Moore, Thomas. (1994). *Care of the soul: A guide for cultivating depth and sacredness in everyday life.* New York: HarperCollins.

Moore, Thomas. (1994). *Soulmates: Honoring the mysteries of love and relationship.* New York: HarperCollins.

Chapter 10: The Art of Conversation

Sacks, H., Schegloff, E. A., & Jefferson, G. (1974). *A simplest systematics for the organization of turn-taking for conversation.* Language, 50, 696-735.

Chapter 12: The Big Picture

Campbell, Joseph. (1972). *Myths to live by.* New York: Viking Press.

photo: Robert H. Miller

About the Author

Patricia Danks has been a marriage and family therapist since 1985. She holds a doctorate in clinical psychology from Pacifica Graduate Institute in Carpinteria, California. An avid student of the psychologist Carl Jung, Danks incorporates his theory of personality and dream interpretation into her individual therapy work. She is an experienced public speaker, often presenting to groups on subjects such as mental health, parenting, women's issues, spirituality, and personal development. Danks practices in Plymouth, Michigan, and lives in nearby Belleville with her husband, John Danks. She has five children, ten grandchildren, and one great grandchild.

Notes

Notes

Notes

Notes